# HOUSEHOLD EDUCATION

## BY

## HARRIET MARTINEAU

# HOUSEHOLD EDUCATION.

## CHAPTER I.

### OLD AND YOUNG IN SCHOOL.

Household education is a subject so important in its bearings on every one's happiness, and so inexhaustible in itself, that I do not see how any person whatever can undertake to lecture upon it authoritatively, as if it was a matter completely known and entirely settled. It seems to me that all that we can do is to reflect, and say what we think, and learn of one another. This is, at least, all that I venture to offer. I propose to say, in a series of chapters, what I have observed and thought on the subject of Life at Home, during upwards of twenty years' study of domestic life in great variety. It will be for my readers to discover whether they agree in my views, and whether their minds are set to work by what I say on a matter which concerns them as seriously as any in the world. Once for all, let me declare here what I hope will be remembered throughout, that I have no ambition to teach; but a strong desire to set members of households consulting together about their course of action towards each other.

It will be seen by these last words that I consider all the members of a household to be going through a process of education together. I am not thinking only of parents drawing their chairs together when the children have gone to bed, to talk over the young people's qualities and ways. That is all very well; but it is only a small part of the business. I am not thinking of the old, experienced grandfather or grandmother talking at the fireside, telling the parents of the sleeping children how they ought to manage them, and what rules and methods were in force in their day. This is all very well; and every sensible person will be thankful to hear what the aged have to tell, out of their long knowledge of life: but this again is a very small part of the matter. Every member of the household—children, servants, apprentices—every inmate of the dwelling, must have a share in the family plan; or those who make it are despots, and those who are excluded are slaves.

Of course, this does not mean that children who have scarcely any knowledge, little judgment, and no experience, are to have a choice about the rules of their own training. The object of training is one thing; and the rules and methods are another. With rules and methods they have nothing to do but to obey them till they become able to command themselves. But there is no rational being who is not capable of understanding, from the time he can speak, what it is to wish to be good. The stupidest servant-girl, and the most thoughtless apprentice-boy, are always impressed by seeing those about them anxious to improve; and especially the oldest of all endeavouring the more to become wiser and wiser, better and better, as their few remaining days dwindle away. If the family plan therefore be the grand comprehensive plan which is alone worthy of people who care about education at all—a plan to do the best that is possible by each other for the improvement of all—every member of the family above the yearling infant must be a member of the domestic school of mutual instruction, and must know that he is so.

It is a common saying that every child thinks his father the wisest man in the world. This is very natural; as parents are their children's fountains of knowledge. To them their children come for anything they want to know: and by them they are generally satisfied. But every wise parent has occasion to say, now and then—"I do not know, my dear." The surprise of the child on first hearing that there is anything that his parents do not know fixes the fact in his mind. When he has once discovered that his parents have something more to learn, he becomes aware —and this also ought to be fixed in his mind—that their education is not finished; and that it is their business, as it is his, to learn something more every day, as long as they live. So much for knowledge. The case ought to be as clear to him with regard to goodness. It is not enough that in church he hears that all men and women are sinners; and that in prayers at home he hears his parents pray that they may become more worthy of the goodness of God, and more like the Christ who is set before them. These things may set him thinking; but there will be, or ought to be, more light every day to clear up his ideas. The same parents who honestly own to their child that they are ignorant of things about which he questions them will own to him that they are not nearly so good as they wish to be. Thus is the truth opened to the feeblest and smallest mind that education has still to go on, even when people are so inconceivably old as children are apt to think their parents.

To us, grown up to this mighty age, there can be no doubt on such a point. We know very well that we are all, through the whole range of society, like a set of ignorant and wayward children, compared with what we are made capable of being. Our best knowledge is but a glimmering—a dawn of light which we may hope will "increase more and more unto the perfect day." Our best goodness is so weak, so mixed, so inferior to what we can conceive of, that we should blush to say that during any day of our lives we had been as good as we ought to be. It is as clear to us as to children, that there is room for improvement in both ways as long as we live. To us there is another question which children cannot enter into, and have no present business with;—whether human beings remain capable of improvement as long as they live.

About this, there are different opinions. I rather think the prevailing belief is that they are not; and that this prevailing belief arises from the commonness of the spectacle, not only of the faults of old age, but of the inability of even amiable and lively old people to receive new ideas, or correct bad habits.

This is certainly the commonest aspect of old age; and serious is the warning it affords to correct our faulty tempers and ways before we grow stiff in mind, as well as in body. But I do not think that this spectacle settles the question. We might as well say that the human intellect can achieve no great work after five-and-twenty, because the ill-educated mind never does. As long as we see one single instance of a mind still expanding in a man of eighty-five, of a temper improving in one of ninety, of a troublesome daily habit conscientiously cured, after the indulgence of a life-time, by an old lady of seventy-five, we perceive that education may go on to the extreme limit of life, and should suppose that it might be generally so, but for the imperfect training of preceding years.

I have known of one old man whose mind was certainly still growing when he died, at the age of eighty-six. I have known of another, whose study through life had been the laws of the mind, and who, when his faculties were failing him, applied himself to that study, marking the gradual decline of certain of his powers, adding the new facts to his stores of knowledge, and thus, nourishing to the last a part of his mind with the decay of the rest. This instance of persevering self-improvement under conditions which any one would admit to be those of release from labour, appears to me even more affecting than that of the great physician who watched his own approaching death with his finger on his pulse, notifying its last beat as his heart came to a stop, hoping to contribute one more fact to useful science. With cases like these before us, how shall we dare to suppose our education completed while we have one faculty remaining, or our hearts have yet one more beat to give?

As for the continuance of moral education to the last, I have seen two contrasted cases, in close neighbourhood, which make the matter pretty plain, in a practical sense, to me. I knew two old ladies, living only the length of a street apart, who were fair specimens of educated and uneducated old age. The one belonged to a family who were remarkable for attaining a great age; and she always confidently reckoned on her lot being the same as that of her predecessors. It is true, her mother, being above a hundred, called her and her sister "the girls" when they were above seventy; but still one would have thought that grey hairs and wrinkles would have gone some way as a warning to her. Instead, however, of reckoning on her future years (if she must reckon on them) as so much time to grow wiser in, she was merely surprised at her friends when they advised her (she being then eighty) to make some other terms for her house than taking another lease of fourteen years. She could not conceive, as the last lease had answered so well, why the next should not. I remember seeing her face, all puckered with wrinkles, surmounted by rows of bright brown false curls, and her arms, bare above the elbows, adorned with armlets, such as young ladies wore half a century before. I remember a clever pert youth setting himself to quiz and amuse her by humouring her in her notions about the state of the world, drawing her out to praise the last century and express her ignorant contempt of this, till she nodded emphatically over her hand of cards, and declared that the depravity of the age was owing to gas-lamps and macadamisation. She died very old, but no wiser than this. Her case proves only that her education did stop; and not that it need have stopped. The other was a woman of no great cultivation, but of a humble, earnest, benevolent nature, full of a sense of duty towards God and man; and, in them, towards herself. Having survived her nearest connections, she had no strong desire to live; and her affairs were always arranged for departure, down to the labelling of every paper, and the neatness of every drawer. Yet no one was more alive to the improvements of the modern world. I shall never forget the earnest look with which she would listen to any tidings of new knowledge, or new social conveniences. A more dignified woman I never knew; yet she listened to the young who brought information—listened as a learner—with a deference which was most touching to witness. But there was more than this. She was conscious of having been, in her earlier days, somewhat hard, somewhat given to lecture and lay down the law, and criticise people all round by family notions; a tendency which, if it really existed, arose from family and not personal pride; for, though she might overrate the wisdom of parents and brothers, there never was any sign of her overvaluing her own. However this might be, she believed that she had been hard and critical in former times; and she went on softening and growing liberal to the day of her death. I never observed any weakness—much less any laxity—in her gentleness towards the feeble and the frail. It was the holy tenderness which the pure and upright can afford to indulge and impart. The crowning proof that her improvement was the result of self-discipline and not of circumstances was that when, at above seventy years of age, she became the inmate of a family whose habits were somewhat rigid, and in many respects unlike her own, she changed her own to suit theirs, even forcing herself to an observance of punctuality, in which she had been deficient all her life, and about which she had scarcely ever needed to think while for many years living alone. Of course, this moral discipline implies some considerable use of the intellect. She read a good deal; and carried an earnest mind into all her pursuits. And when her memory began to fail, and she could not retain beyond the day what she had read, her mind did not become weak. It was always at work, and always on good subjects, though she could no longer add much to her store of mere knowledge. Her case proves surely that education need never stop.

Now, if we picture to ourselves a household, with an honoured being like this as the occupant of the fireside chair, we can at once see how it may be completely understood and agreed upon among them all that the education of every one of them is always going on, and to go on for ever while they live. No child could ever stand at the knee of my old friend without feeling that she was incessantly bent on self-improvement—as earnest to learn from the humblest and youngest as ready to yield the benefits of her experience and reflections to any whom she could inform and guide. When taken severely ill, she said with a smile, to one by her bedside, "Why do you look so anxious? If I do die to-day, there is nothing to be unhappy about. I have long passed the time when I expected to go. What does it matter whether I die now or a twelve-month hence?" And when that illness was over, she regarded it as a process in her training, and persevered, as before, in trying to grow wiser and more worthy. Here was a case in which Household Education visibly included the oldest as naturally as the youngest. And in all dwellings, all the members are included in the influences which work upon the whole, whether they have the wisdom to see it or not. Henceforward, therefore, I shall write on the supposition that we are all children together—from the greatest to the least—the wisest and the best needing all the good they can get from the peculiar influences of Home.

# CHAPTER II.

## WHAT THE SCHOOLING IS FOR.

Every home being a school for old and young together, it is necessary, if the training is to be a good one, to be clear as to what the schooling is for.

For the improvement of the pupils, is the most obvious answer.

Yes; but what do you mean by improvement? We must settle what we want to make of the pupils, or everything will go on at random. In every country of the world there is some sort of general notion of what the men and women in it ought to be: and the men and women turn out accordingly: and the more certainly, the more clear the notion is.

The patriarchs, some thousands of years ago, had very clear notions of their own of what people ought to be. One of these sitting in the evening of a hot day under a terebinth tree ten times his own age, would be able to give a distinct account of what he would have the training of his great-grandchildren tend to. He would lay it down as the first point of all that the highest honour and the greatest privilege in the world was to be ex tremely old. The next most desirable thing was to have the largest possible number of descendants; because the earth was very wide, with not half enough people in it; and the more people a patriarch had about him, the richer and more beautiful would the valleys and pastures be, and the more power and authority he would have—every patriarch being an absolute ruler over his own family, and the more like a king the larger his tribe. Of course, the old man would say decidedly that to make the best possible man you must train a child to obey his parents, and yet more the head of the tribe, with the most absolute submission; to do in the cleverest way what was necessary for defence against an enemy, and to obtain food, and the skins of beasts for clothing. The more wives and the more children the better. These were the principal points. After these, he would speak of its being right for such as would probably become the head of a tribe to cultivate such wisdom and temper as would make them good rulers, and enable them to maintain peace among their followers. Such was the patriarchal notion of improving a man to the utmost—omitting certain considerations which we think important,—truthfulness, temperance, amiability, respect for other men, and reverence for something a good deal more solemn than mere old age.

Some wise men in Greece would have given a different account of the aim of Education. A Spartan, for instance, living in a little country which was always in danger from enemies without and slaves within, looked upon every boy as a future soldier, and as born to help to preserve the state. Every sickly or deformed child might be killed off at the desire of his father's kin. The healthy and promising were looked after by the state from their earliest years; and at the age of seven were put under public training entirely. They were taught to bear hunger, and be content with coarse food; to endure flogging without a groan, sometimes to the point of death; and all for practice in bearing pain. They were trained to all warlike exercises; their amusements were wrestling and sham battles; their accomplishments singing martial songs. They were taught to reverence rank and age; to hate their enemies; to use fraud in war; to be unable to bear shame, whether deserved or not; and to treat women with respect, not at all for their own sakes, but because despised women could not be the mothers of heroes. Thus, to make a perfect soldier was what a good Spartan considered the great object of education.

The Jew in his own Palestine would have given a different answer, in some respects, though he also reared his children to hate their enemies, and to covet both martial and patriarchal glory. His leading belief was that a greater God than any other nation had ever worshipped was the special ruler and protector of his own. Jehovah was the king as well as the God of the Jews; and the first virtue of a Jew was to obey every tittle of the Law, which ordered all things whatsoever in the lives of those who lived under it. Obedience to the Law, in affairs of food, dress, seasons of work, sleep, worship, journeying, &c., as well as in some higher matters, was the main thing taught by a good parent, while he knew and thought nothing of the higher and holier aims opened by the Gospel; of which, indeed, many a well-meaning Jewish parent could not bear to hear from the lips of Christ, when he came to declare what every man should be. When he declared that men should rise above the Law, and be perfect as their Father in Heaven is perfect, some strict Jewish educators crucified him. In a Jew's mind, the best man was he who most servilely obeyed the letter of the Law.

When I was in America, I saw three kinds of people who had their own notions of what it was to be a perfect man—each their own idea of the chief aim in Education; notions as wide of each other as those of the Patriarch, the Spartan, and the Jew. There were the dwellers in the cities; men speaking our language, and looking very like ourselves. These men were, as was natural, proud of their young and prosperous republic; and they thought more about politics than appears to us necessary or wise in a life which contains so many other great interests. Their children were brought up to talk politics before they could be qualified to have an opinion; and taught at school to despise other nations, and glorify their own, as a preparation for exercising the suffrage at twenty-one, and thereby becoming, in a republic so constituted, a member of the government. The privilege—the trust—is a most important one; and we cannot wonder that the subject is an engrossing one to parents and children. The object of education among a very large proportion of American parents is to make politicians: and it certainly is attained.

On the same continent, I saw something of a very different race—the red men. Their idea of perfection is a man's being a perfect warrior; and yet in a way quite unlike the Spartans. The red Indian is not trained as a servant of the State, but as an individual: and the Indian women are degraded and oppressed, while the Spartan women were considered and respected—whatever the ground of consideration might be. The Indian boy is trained to use his five senses till they reach an unequalled degree of nicety. And, when old enough to bear the pain without dying, he is subjected first to hunger and want of sleep, and then to such horrible tortures as it turns one sick to think of. He who comes out of this trial the most bravely, and who afterwards shows himself the most alert sentinel, the strongest and most enduring soldier, the most revengeful enemy, the most cruel conqueror, and the sternest husband and father, is, in the eyes of his people, the most perfect man. The red Indians, therefore, generally make an approach to this kind of character.

In the island of Mackinaw lives the other sort of people I have referred to. This island rises out of the wide waters of the great northern lakes, a perfect paradise in the midst of the boundless blue expanse. The people who inhabit it are, for the most part, half-breeds—the offspring of the red race and the French colonists who first settled on the island. The great object here seems to be to become amphibious; and truly, it appeared to me pretty well attained. The dark-skinned boys who surrounded our ship, and all others that I saw, were poppling about in the water, as easily as so many fowl: and they scud about in their tiny birch-bark canoes as readily as we walk on our feet, thinking no more of being capsized than we do of falling.

The aim here has about the same level as that of the Arabs, to whom water is the greatest rarity, and to whom the sandy desert serves much the same purpose as the inland seas to the dwellers in Mackinaw. The horse of the Arab is to him as the bark-canoe to the half-breed of Mackinaw: and children are launched into the desert, to live in it as they best may, as the half-breed boys are into the watery waste. And they succeed as well, conquering the desert, turning its dangers into sport, and making a living out of it. And so it is with the native dwellers in the icy deserts of Siberia. A perfectly educated person there is one who can surprise the greatest number of water-fowl in summer, foretell soonest the snow storm in winter, best learn the hour from the stars, bank up the most sheltered sleeping-place in the snow, and light a fire within it the most quickly; dive among the beavers for the longest time; see in the dark like an owl, track game like a pointer, fetch it like a spaniel, hearken like a deer, and run like an ostrich.

Such being the Mongolian notion of perfection, it is more nearly approached by them than by others.

None of these aims are ours, or such as we approve. What then is ours? It is easy to answer, "to grow wiser and better every day:" but then comes the question, what is the wisdom, what is the goodness, that we aspire to? All the people I have mentioned aim at improvement in wisdom and goodness every day. Our difference with them is precisely about what wisdom and goodness are.

We are not likely to agree by setting up each our own notion of wisdom and goodness. Hear children at school talking of the heroes they admire most, and see how seldom they agree. One admires the brave man; another the patient man; another the philanthropist; another the man of power; another the man of holiness; another the patriot. Hear men talking by the fireside of the sages of the race; how they vary in their preferences, and select for themselves from among the group of mighty minds—the fathers of philosophy, of science, of art, of law and government, of morals. We shall never arrive at a practical point by setting up our separate preferences as aims for all.

Nor will it answer to fix our aim by any single example: no, not even—with reverence be it spoken—by the great Exemplar, Christ himself. The fault and weakness of this inability are in ourselves. It is not any cloud in him, but partial blindness in us, which renders this method insufficient by itself. All-perfect as is the example, we cannot all, and constantly, use its full perfection, from our tendency to contemplate it from the favourite point of view which every one of us has. One of us dwells most on the tenderness of his character; another on its righteous sternness; one on his power; another on his meek patience; and so on. And thus, while it is, and ever will be, of the utmost importance that we should preserve the aim of becoming like Christ, it yet remains to be settled among us, in fact though not perhaps in words, what Christ was, the images of him in different minds varying so endlessly as they certainly do.

The only method that appears to me absolutely safe and wise, is one which perfectly well agrees with our taking this great Exemplar as our model. Each of us has a frame, "fearfully and wonder fully made;" with such a variety of powers, that no one yet knows them all, or can be sure that he understands the extent of any one of them. It is impossible that we can be wrong in desiring and endeavouring to bring out and strengthen and exercise all the powers given to every human being. In my opinion, this should be the aim of education.

I have said "to bring out, and strengthen, and exercise all the powers." Some would add, "and balance them." But if all were faithfully exercised, I am of opinion that a better balance would ensue than we could secure, so partial as are our views, and so imperfect as has been the training of the best of us.

I shall gladly proceed, in my next chapter, to declare what I think we have learned as to what the powers of the human being are. At present, I can only just point out that the aim proposed is superior to every other mentioned, and I believe to any other that can be mentioned for this reason; that it applies universally—meets every case that can be conceived of. In the patriarch's scheme of education, the women—half the race—were slighted. In the Spartan system, the slaves and all work-people were left out. Among the modern republicans, citizens have the preference over women and slaves: and under the savage training—the Indian, Arab, and Mongolian—no individual whatever is done justice to. And there is not a country in Christendom where equal justice is done to all those whom we see entering the world so endowed as that we ought to look on every one of them with religious awe as a being too noble for our estimate. The aim proposed—of doing justice to all the powers of every human being under training—includes all alike, and must therefore be just. It includes women, the poor, the infirm—all who were rejected or slighted under former systems—while it does more for the privileged than any lower principle ever proposed to do. It appears that under it none will be the worse, but all the better, in comparison of this with any lower aim.

To obtain a clearer and firmer notion of what this object really comprehends, we must next make out, as well as our present knowledge allows, what the powers of the human being are. I mean as to their kind; for I do not think any one will venture to say what is the extent of endowments so vast; and in their vastness so obscure.

# CHAPTER III.

## THE NATURAL POSSESSIONS OF MAN.

What are the powers of the human being?

I speak of those powers only which are the object of education. There are some which work of themselves for the preservation of life, and with which we have nothing to do but to let them work freely. The heart beats, the stomach digests, the lungs play, the skin transpires, without any care of ours, and we have only to avoid hindering any of these actions.

Next, man has four limbs. Of these, two have to be trained to move him from place to place in a great variety of ways. There are many degrees of agility between the bow-legged cripple, set too early upon his feet, and the chamois hunter of the Alps, who leaps the icy chasms of the glacier, and springs from point to point of the rock. The two seem hardly to be of the same race; yet education has made each of them what he is.

The two other limbs depend upon training for much of their strength and use. Look at the pale student, who lives shut up in his study, never having been trained to use his arms and hands but for dressing and feeding himself, turning over books, and guiding the pen. Look at his spindles of arms and his thin fingers, and compare them with the brawny limbs of the blacksmith, or the hands of the quay porter, whose grasp is like that of a piece of strong machinery. Compare the feeble and awkward touch of the book-worm who can hardly button his waistcoat, or carry his cup of tea to his mouth, with the power that the modeller, the ivory carver, and the watchmaker have over their fingers. It is education which has made the difference between these.

Man has five senses. Though much is done by the incidents of daily life to exercise all the five, still a vast difference ensues upon varieties of training. A fireman in London, and an Indian in the prairie, can smell smoke when nobody else is aware of it. An epicure can taste a cork in wine, or a spice in a stew, to the dismay of the butler, and the delight of the cook, when every one else is insensible. One person can feel by the skin whether the wind is east or west before he gets out of bed in the morning; while another has to hold up a handkerchief in the open air, or look at the weathercock, before he can answer the question—"How's the wind?"

As for the two noblest senses, there are great constitutional differences among men. Some are naturally short-sighted, and some dull of hearing; but the differences caused by training are more frequent and striking. If, of two boys born with equally good eyes and ears, one is very early put, all alone, to keep sheep on a hill side, where he never speaks or is spoken to, and comes home only to sleep, and the other works with his father at joiner's work, or in sea-fishing, or at a water-mill, they will, at manhood, hardly appear to belong to the same race. While the one can tell veneer from mahogany in passing a shop-window, the other cannot see any difference between one stranger's face and another's. While the sleepy clown cannot distinguish sea from land half a mile off, the fisherman can see the greyest sail of the smallest sloop among the billows on the horizon. While the shepherd does not hear himself called till the shout is in his ear, the miller tells by the fireside, by the run of the water, whether the stream is deepening or threatening to go dry. Of course, the quickness or slowness of the mind has much to do with these differences of eye and ear; but besides that, the eye and ear differ according to training. The miller, with his mind and ear all awake, would hear, with all his efforts, only four or five birds' notes in a wood, where a naturalist would hear twenty; and the fisherman might declare the wide air to be vacant, when a mountain sportsman would see an eagle, like a minute speck, indicating by its mode of flight where the game lay below.

Man has a capacity for pleasure and pain.

This is an all-important part of his nature of which we can give no account, because it is incomprehensible. How he feels pleasure and pain, and why one sensation or thought delights him and another makes him miserable, nobody ever knew yet, or perhaps ever will know. It is enough for us that the fact is so. Of all the solemn considerations involved in the great work of education, none is so awful as this—the right exercise and training of the sense of pleasure and pain. The man who feels most pleasure in putting brandy into his stomach, or in any other way gratifying his nerves of sensation, is a mere beast. One whose chief pleasure is in the exercise of the limbs, and who plays without any exercise of the mind, is a more harmless sort of animal, like the lamb in the field, or the swallow skimming over meadow or pool. He whose delight is to represent nature by painting, or to build edifices by some beautiful idea, or to echo feelings in music, is of an immeasurably higher order. Higher still is he who is charmed by thought, above everything—whose understanding gives him more satisfaction than any other power he has. Higher still is he who is never so happy as when he is making other people happy—when he is relieving pain, and giving pleasure to two, or three, or more people about him. Higher yet is he whose chief joy it is to labour at great and eternal thoughts, in which lies bound up the happiness of a whole nation and perhaps a whole world, at a future time when he will be mouldering in his grave. Any man who is capable of this joy, and at the same time of spreading comfort and pleasure among the few who live round about him, is the noblest human being we can conceive of. He is also the happiest. It is true that his capacity for pain is exercised and enlarged, as well as his power of feeling pleasure. But what pains such a man is the vice, and folly, and misery of his fellow-men; and he knows that these must melt away hereafter in the light of the great ideas which he perceives to be in store for them: while his pleasure being in the faith of a better future is as vivid and as sure as great thoughts are clear and eternal. For an illustration of this noblest means of happiness, we had better look to the highest instance of all. I have always thought that we are apt to dwell too much on the suffering and sorrow of the lot and mind of Christ. Our reverence and sympathy should be more with his abounding joy. I think those who read with clear eyes and an open mind will see evidences of an unutterable joy in his words—may almost think they hear it in his tones, when he promised heaven to the disinterested and earth to the meek, and satisfaction to the earnest; when he welcomed the faith of the centurion, and the hope of the penitent, and the charity of the widow; when he foresaw the incoming of the Gentiles, and knew that heaven and earth should pass away sooner than his words of life and truth. The sufferings of the holy can never surely transcend their peace: and whose fulness of joy can compare with theirs?

Before man can feel pleasure or pain from outward objects or from thoughts, he must perceive them. To a new-born infant, or a blind person enabled to see for the first time, objects before the eyes can hardly be said to exist. The blue sky and a green tree beside a white house are not seen but as a blotch of colours which touches the eye. This is the account given by persons couched for cataract, who have never before seen a ray of light. They see as if they saw not. But the power is in them. By degrees they receive the images, and perceive the objects. A child learns to receive sounds separately; then to perceive one voice among others; then to distinguish one tone from another—the voice of soothing from that of playfulness—the tone of warning from that of approbation; then it receives thoughts through the sounds; and so on, till the power is exercised to the fullest extent that we know of—when distinct ideas are admitted from the minutest appearances or leadings—strange bodies detected in the heavens, and fresh truths in the loftiest regions of human speculation. It depends much on training whether objects and thoughts remain for life indistinct and confused before the perceptive power, as before infant vision, or whether all is clear and vivid as before a keen and practised eye.

We know not how Memory acts, any more than we understand how we feel pleasure and pain. But we all know how the power of recalling images, words, thoughts, and feelings, depends on exercise. A person whose power of memory has been neglected has little use of his past life. The time, and people, and events that have passed by have left him little better than they found him: while every day, every person, and every incident deposits some wealth of knowledge with him whose memory can receive and retain his experience.

Then there are other powers which it will be enough merely to mention here, as we shall have to consider them more fully hereafter. Man has the power, after perceiving objects and thoughts, to compare them, and see when they differ and agree; to penetrate their nature, and understand their purpose and action. It is thus that he obtains a knowledge of creation, and the curious powers, whether hidden or open to view, which are for ever at work in it.

He can reason from what he knows to what he has reason to suppose, and put his idea to the proof. He can imitate what he sees; and also the idea in his mind; and hence comes invention; and that wise kind of guess into what is possible which leads to great discovery; discovery sometimes of a vast continent, sometimes of a vast agency in nature for men's uses, sometimes of a vast truth which may prove a greater acquisition to men's souls than a new hemisphere for their habitation.

Man has also a wonderful power of conceiving of things about which he cannot reason. We do not know how it is, but the more we dwell on what is beautiful and striking, what is true before our eyes and impressive to our minds, the more able we become to conceive of things more beautiful, striking, and noble, which have never existed, but might well be true. None of our powers require more earnest and careful exercise than this grand one of the Imagination. Those in whom it is suppressed can never be capable of heroic acts, of lofty wisdom, of the purest happiness. Those in whom it is neglected may exercise the little power they have in a fruitless direction, probably aggravating their own faults, and certainly wasting the power on ideas too low for it, as the voluptuary who dreams of selfish pleasure, or the despot, grand or petty, who makes visions of unchecked tyranny. Those in whom it is healthily exercised will become as elevated and expanded as their nature admits, and one here and there proves a Mahommed, lifting up half the human race into a higher condition; or a Raffaelle, bringing down seraphs and cherubs from heaven, and so clothing them as that men may look upon them and grow like them; or a Shakspere who became a creator in that way which is truly no impiety, but, on the contrary, the highest worship. Men are apt, in all times and everywhere, to blaspheme, by attributing to God their own evil passions and narrow ideas. It is through this power of the Imagination that they rise to that highest ideal which is the truest piety. They rise to share godlike attributes; the prophet seeing "the things that are not as though they were," and the poet creating beings that live and move and have their being, immortal in the mind of man. Such a power resides more or less in every infant that lies in the bosom of every family. Alas for its guardians if they quench this power, or turn it into a curse and disease by foul feeding!

Then, the Emotions of men are so many powers, to be recognised and trained. Of the power of Hope there is no need to speak, for all see what it is as a stimulus, both in particular acts, and through the whole course of a life. Fear is hardly less important, though it is intended to die out, or rather to pass into other and higher kinds of feeling. A child who has never known a sensation of fear (if there be such an one) can never be a man of a high order. He must either be coarsely made in body, or unable to conceive of anything but what is familiar to him. A child whose heart beats at shadows and the fitful sounds of the invisible wind, and who hides his face on his mother's bosom when the stars seem to be looking at him as they roll, is no philosopher at present; but he is likely to grow into one if this fear is duly trained into awe, humility, thoughtfulness, till, united with knowledge, it becomes contemplation, and grows into that glorious courage which searches all through creation for ultimate truth. Out of Fear, too, grows our power of Pity. Without fear of pain, we could not enter into the pain of others. Fear must be lost in reverence and love: but reverence and love could never be so powerful as they ought to be, if they were not first vivified by the power of Fear.

What the power of Love is, in all its forms, there is no need to declare to any one who has an eye and a heart. In the form of Pity, how it led Howard to spend his life in loathsome prisons, crowded with yet more loathsome guilt! In other forms, how it sustains the unwearied mother watching through long nights over her wailing infant! How it makes of a father, rough perhaps to all others, a holy and tender guardian of his pure daughters! and how it makes ministering angels of them to him in turn! How we see it, everywhere in the world, making the feeble and otherwise scantily-endowed strong in self-denial, cheerful to endure, fearless to die! A mighty power surely is that which, breathing from the soul of an individual man, can "conquer Death, and triumph over Time."

Then there is in man a force by which he can win and conquer his way through all opposition of circumstance, and the same force in others. This power of Will is the greatest force on earth—the most important to the individual, and the most influential over the whole race. A strong Will turned to evil lets hell loose upon the world. A strong Will wholly occupied with good might do more than we can tell to bring down Heaven into the midst of us. If among all the homes of our land, there be one infant in whom this force is discerned working strongly, and if that infant be under such guardianship as to have its will brought to bear on things that are pure, holy, and lovely, to that being we may look as to a regenerator of his race. He may be anywhere where there are children. Are there any parents who will not look reverently into the awful nature of their children, search into their endowments, and try of every one of them whether it may not be he? If not he, it is certain that every one of them is a being too mysterious, too richly gifted, and too noble in faculties not to be welcomed and cherished as a heaven-sent stranger. How can we too carefully set in order the home in which it is to dwell?

# CHAPTER IV.

## HOW TO EXPECT.

Whatever method parents may choose for educating a child, they must have some idea in their minds of what they would have him turn out. Even if they set before them the highest aim of all—exercising and training all his powers—still they must have some thoughts and wishes, some hopes and fears, as to what the issue will prove to be.

In all states of society, the generality of parents have wished that their children should turn out such as the opinion of their own time and country should approve. There is a law of opinion in every society as to what people should be. We have seen something of what this opinion was among the Patriarchs of old, the Spartans, the Jews, and others. In our own day, we find wide differences among neighbouring nations, civilised, and so-called, christianised. The French have a greater value for kindness and cheerfulness of temper and manners than the English, and a less value for truth. The Russians have a greater value for social order and obedience, and less for honesty. The Americans have a greater value for activity of mind and pursuits, and less for peace and comfort. In these and all other countries, parents in general will naturally desire that their children should turn out that which is taken for granted to be most valuable.

An ordinary English parent of our time, who had not given much thought to the subject, would wish that his son should turn out as follows. He would wish that the child should be docile and obedient, clever enough to make teaching him an easy matter, and to afford promise of his being a distinguished man; truthful, affectionate, and spirited; that as a man he should be upright and amiable, sufficiently religious to preserve his tranquillity of mind and integrity of conduct: steady in his business and prudent in his marriage, so far as to be prosperous in his affairs.

Now, this looks all very well to a careless eye: but it will not satisfy a thoughtful mind. In all the ages and societies we have spoken of, there have been a few men wiser than the average, who have seen that the human being might and ought to be something better than the law of Opinion required that he should be. There are certainly Hindoos now living and meditating who do not consider that men are so good as they might be, while they think no harm of lying and stealing, and who are sorry for the superstition which makes it an unpardonable crime to hurt a cow. There are men among the Americans who see virtue in repose of mind, and moderation of desires to which the majority of their countrymen are insensible. And so it is in our country. We are all agreed, from end to end of society, that Truthfulness, Integrity, Courage, Purity, Industry, Benevolence, and a spirit of Reverence for sacred things are inexpressibly desirable and excellent. But when it comes to the question of the degree of these good things which it is desirable to attain, we find the difference between the opinion of the many and that of the higher few. A being who had these qualities in the highest degree could not get on in our existing society without coming into conflict with our law of Opinion at almost every step. If he were perfectly truthful, he must say and do things in the course of his business which would make him wondered at and disliked; he might be unable to take an oath, or enter into any sort of vow, or sell his goods prosperously, or keep on good terms with bad neighbours. If he were perfectly honourable and generous, he might find it impossible to trade or labour on the competitive principle, and might thus find himself helpless and despised among a busy and wealth-gathering society. If he were perfectly courageous, he might find himself spurned for cowardice in declining to go to war or fight a duel. If he were perfectly pure, he might find himself rebuked and pitied for avoiding a mercenary marriage, and entering upon one which brings with it no advantage of connexion or money. If the same purity should lead him to see that though the virtue of chastity cannot be overrated, it has, for low purposes, been made so prominent as to interfere with others quite as important: if he should see how thus a large proportion of the girlhood of England is plunged into sin and shame, and then excluded from all justice and mercy; if, seeing this, he is just and merciful to the fallen, it is probable that his own respectability will be impeached, and that some stain of impurity will be upon his name. If he is perfectly industrious, strenuously employing his various faculties upon important objects, he will be called an idler in comparison with those who work in only one narrow track; as an eminent author of our time was accused by the housemaid, who was for ever dusting the house, of "wasting his time a-writing and reading so much." Just so the majority of men who have one sort of work to do accuse him of idleness who has more directions for his industry than they can comprehend. If he is perfectly benevolent, he cannot hope to be considered a prudent, orderly, quiet member of society. He will be either incessantly spreading himself abroad, and spending himself in the service of all about him, or maturing in retirement some plan of rectification which will be troublesome to existing interests. If he be perfectly reverent in soul, looking up to the loftiest subjects of human contemplation with an awe too deep and true to admit any mixture of either levity or superstition, he will probably be called an infidel; or at least, a dangerous person, for not passively accepting the sayings of men instead of searching out the truth by the faithful use of his own powers.

Thus we see how in our own, as in every other society, the law of Opinion as to what men should be agrees in the large, general points of character with the ideas of the wisest, while there are great differences in the practical management of men's lives. The perplexity to many thoughtful parents is what to wish and aim at.

Now, it must never be forgotten that it is a good thing that there must everywhere be such a law of Opinion on this subject, though it necessarily falls below the estimate of the wisest. Some rule and method in the rearing of human beings there must be; and if some are dwarfed under it, many more have a better chance than they would have if it were not a settled matter that truth, courage, benevolence, &c., are good things. Till the constitution and training of the human being are better and more extensively understood than they are, the general rule is something to go by, as the product of a general instinct; and it will work upon nearly all those who are born under it, so as to bring them into something like order. In our country, there is, I suppose, scarcely a den so dark as that its inhabitants really think no harm whatever of lying and stealing, or consider them merits, as is the case in some parts of the world. While we have among us far too many who thieve and cheat, and quarrel, and drink, we can scarcely meet with any who do not think these things wrong, or have not thought so before they were too far gone in them. On the whole, the law of Opinion, though far below what the wise see it might be, is a great benefit, and a thing worthy of serious regard in fixing our educational aims.

This prevalent opinion being a good thing as far as it goes, having its origin in nature, there can be no doubt that a good education, having also its origin in nature, would issue in a sufficient accordance with it for purposes of social happiness. As human beings are born with limbs and senses whose thorough exercise brings them out in a high state of bodily perfection, they are born with powers of the brain which, thoroughly exercised, would, in like manner, bring them out as great, mentally and morally, as their constitution enables them to be. There must ever be innumerable varieties, as no two infants could ever be said to be born perfectly alike; and perhaps no two adults could be found who had precisely the same powers of limb and sense: but out of this infinite variety must come such an amount of evidence as to what is best in human character as would constitute a law of Opinion, higher than the present, but agreeing with it in its main points. Let us conceive of a county of England where every inhabitant should be not only saved from ignorance, but having every power of body and mind made the very most of. The variety would appear much greater than anything we now see. There would be more people decidedly musical, or decidedly mechanical, or decidedly scientific: more who would occupy their lives with works of benevolence, or of art, or of ingenuity: more who would speculate boldly, speak eloquently, and show openly their high opinion of themselves, or their anxiety for the good opinion of others. The more variety and the greater strength of powers, the clearer would be the evidence before all eyes of what is really the most to be desired for men. It would come out more plainly than now that it is a bad and unhappy thing for men to have immoderate desires for money, or luxury, or fame, or to have quarrelsome tendencies, or to be subject to distrust and jealousy of others, or to be afraid of pain of body or mind. It would be more plain than ever that there is a soulfelt charm and nobleness and happiness in a spirit of reverence, of justice, of charity, of domestic attachment, and of devotion to truth. Thus, in such a society, there would be an agreement, more clear and strong than now, in all the best points of our present law of Opinion, while there would be fuller scope for carrying up the highest qualities of the human being to their perfection.

Moreover, as men are made every where with a general likeness of the powers of the mind, as with the same number of limbs and senses, there must come out of a thorough exercise of their faculties a sufficient agreement as to what is best to generate a universal idea of duty or moral good. No varieties of endowment can interfere essentially with this result. The Hindoo has slender arms, with soft muscles, and cannot do the hard work which suits the German peasant: yet both agree as to what arms are for, and how they are to be used. The Red Indian can see, hear, smell, and taste twice as well as factory children or plough-boys; yet all will agree that it is a good thing to have perfect sight and hearing. And, in the same way, the African may have less power of thought than the Englishman; and the Englishman may have less genius for music than the African: but not only is the African able to think, more or less, and the Englishman to enjoy music, but they will agree that it is a good thing to have the highest power of thought, and the greatest genius for music. In the same manner, again, one race, as well as one individual, may have more power of reverence, another of love, another of self-reliance; but all will agree that all these are inestimably good.

It follows from this, that parents must be safe in aiming at thoroughly exercising and training all the powers of a child. If it would be safest for all to do so, in the certainty that the result would be in accordance with the best points of the law of Opinion, it must be a safe practice for individuals; and they may proceed in the faith that their work (if they do it well) will turn out a noble one in the eyes of the men of their own day, while they are doing their best to help on a clearer and brighter day, when the law of Opinion will itself be greatly ennobled.

Here I must end my chapter. But I must just say a word to guard against any hasty supposition that when I speak of exercising (as well as training) all the human powers thoroughly, I contemplate any indulgence of strong passions or of evil inclinations. It cannot be too carefully remembered that what I am speaking of is human Powers or Faculties; and that every power which a human being possesses may be exercised to good, and is actually necessary to make him perfect.

It will be my business hereafter to show what this exercise and training should be.

# CHAPTER V.

## THE GOLDEN MEAN.

It is a large subject that we have to treat;—that of household education; for the main part of every process of education is carried on at home, except in the instance of boarding-schools, where a few years are spent by a small number of the youth of our country. The queen was brought up under a method of household education; and so was, no doubt, the last pauper who went to his grave in a workhouse coffin. Elizabeth Fry was brought up at home; so was the most ignorant and brutish convict that was blessed by the saving light of her pitying eye. Sir Isaac Newton, to whom the starry heavens were as a home-field for intellectual exercises, was reared at home; and so were the poor children in the Durham coal-pits in our own time, who never heard of God, and indeed could not tell the names of their own fathers and mothers. If thus, the loftiest and the lowliest, the purest and the most criminal, the wisest and the most ignorant, are comprehended under the process of household education, what a wide and serious subject it is that we have to consider!

The royal child must, of course, be trained wholly at home; that is, little princes and princesses cannot be sent to school. But, while reared in the house with their parents, the influences they are under scarcely agree with our ideas of home. The royal infant does not receive its food from the bosom first, or afterwards from the hands of its mother. She does not wash and dress it; and those sweet seasons are lost which in humbler homes are so rich in caresses and play, so fruitful in endearing influences both to mother and child. It is a thing to be remarked and praised by a whole court, if not a whole kingdom, if a royal mother is seen with her child in her arms; while the cottager's child is blessed with countless embraces between morning and night, and sleeps on its mother's arm or within reach of her eye and voice. The best trained royal child is disciplined to command of temper and manners; made to do little services for people about him, and sedulously taught that a child should be humble and docile. But the young creature is all the while taught stronger lessons by circumstances than can ever come through human lips. He sees that a number of grown persons about him are almost wholly occupied with him, and that it is their business in life to induce him to command his temper and manners. He feels that when he is bid to fetch and carry, or to do any other little service, it is not because such service is wanted, but for the sake of the training to himself. He is aware that all that concerns him every day is a matter of arrangement, and not of necessity; and a want of earnestness and of steady purpose is an inevitable consequence. This want of natural stimulus goes into his studies. I believe no solitary child gets on well with book-learning as a part of the business of every day. The best tutors, the best books, the quietest school-room, will not avail, if the child's mind be not stirred and interested by something more congenial than the grammar and sums and maps he has to study. And every royal child is solitary, however many brothers and sisters he may have older and younger than himself. He has his own servants, his own tutor, his own separate place and people, so that he can never be jostled among other children, or lead the true life of childhood. And so proceeds the education of life for him. He can never live amidst a large class of equals, with whom he can measure his powers, and from among whom he may select congenial friends. He passes his life in the presence of servants, has no occupations and no objects actually appointed to him, unless his state be that of sovereignty, in which case his position is more unfavourable still. He dies at last in the midst of that habitual solitude which disables him from conceiving, even at such a moment, of the state in which "rich and poor lie down together." Such a being may, if the utmost has been done for him, be decent in his habits, amiable in temper and manners, innocent in his pursuits, and religious in his feelings; but it is inconceivable that he can ever approach to our idea of a perfect man, with an intellect fully exercised, affections thoroughly disciplined, and every faculty educated by those influences which arise only from equal intercourse with men at large.

The home education of the pauper child is no better, though there are few who would venture to say how much worse it is. A pauper child must (I think we may say) be unfortunate in its parentage, in one way or another. If it knows its parents, they must probably be either sickly, or foolish, or idle, or dissolute; or they would not be in a state of permanent pauperism. The infant is reared (if not in the workhouse) in some unwholesome room or cellar, amidst damp and dirt, and the noises and sights of vice or folly. He is badly nursed and fed, and grows up feeble, or in a state of bodily uneasiness which worries his temper, and makes his passions excitable. He is not soothed by the constant tenderness of a decent mother, who feels it a great duty to make him as good and happy as she can, and contrives to find time and thought for that object. He tumbles in the dust of the road or the mud of the gutter, snatches food wherever he can get it, quarrels with anybody who thwarts him if he be a bold boy, and sneaks and lies if he be naturally a coward. He indulges every appetite, as a matter of course, as it arises; for he has no idea that he should not. He hates everybody who interferes with this license, and has the best liking for those who use the same license with himself. He knows nothing of any place or people but those he sees, and never dreams of any world beyond that of his own eyes. He does not know what society is, or law, or duty: and therefore, when he injures society, and comes under the inflictions of the law for gross violations of duty, he understands no more of what is done to him than if he was carried through certain ceremonies conducted in an unknown tongue. He has some dim notion of glory in dying boldly before the eyes of the crowd; so he goes to the gallows in a mocking mood, as ignorant of the true import of life and human faculties as the day he was born. Or, if not laid hold of by the law, he goes on towards his grave brawling and drinking, or half asleep in mind, and inert or diseased in body, till at last he dies as the beast dies.

Here are the two extremes. The condition about half way between them appears to me to be the most favourable, on the whole, for making the most of a human being, and best fulfilling the purposes of his life. There are stations above and below highly favourable to the attainment of excellence; but, taking in all considerations, I think the position of the well-conditioned artisan the most favourable that society affords, at least, in our own day.

There is much good in enlarged book-learning; in what is commonly called a liberal education. If united with hard and imperative labour—labour at once of head and hands—it will help to make a nobler man than can be made without it: but a liberal education, enlarged book-learning, ordinarily leads to only head work, without that labour of the hands which is the way to much wisdom. The benefits too are much confined to the individual, so that the children of the wisest statesman, or physician, or lawyer are only accidentally, if at all, the better for his advantages; while the best circumstances in the lot of the well-conditioned artisan are the inheritance and the privilege of his children.

And again, the labourer may be so placed, in regard to employment, marriage, and abode, as that he may, possessing an awakened mind, be for ever learning great and interesting things from the book of Nature and of Scripture, while he has comfort in his home, and some leisure for training his children to his own work, and whatever else may turn up, so that they may grow up intelligent, dutiful, affectionate, and able continually to improve. The surgeon, the manufacturer, and the shop-keeper on the one hand, and the street porter, the operative, and the labourer on the other, may well work out the true purposes of life; but the condition which appears to me to be the meeting point of the greatest number of good influences is that of the best order of artisans.

That condition affords the meeting point of book-knowledge, and that which is derived from personal experience. Every day's labour of hand and eye is a page opened in the best of books—the universe. When duly done, this lesson leaves time for the other method of instruction, by books. During the day hours, the earnest pupil learns of Nature by the lessons she gives in the melting fire, the rushing water, the unseen wind, the plastic metal or clay, the variegated wood or marble, the delicate cotton, silk, or wool; and at evening he learns of men—of the wise and genial men who have delivered the best parts of their minds in books, and made of them a sort of ethereal vehicle, in which they can come at a call to visit any secret mind which desires communion with them. And this privilege of double instruction is one which extends to the whole household of the chief pupil. The children of the artisan are happily appointed, without room for doubt, to toil like their father; and there is every probability that they will share his opportunity and his respect for book-knowledge. At the outset of life, they are tended by their mother, owing directly to her their food and clothes, their lullaby and their incitement to play. During the day, they are under her eye; and in the evening, they sit on their father's knee, and get knowledge or fun from him. In their busy home, all the help is needed that every one can give; so the real business of life begins early, and with it the most natural and best discipline. The children learn that it is an honour to be useful, and a comfort and blessing to be neat and industrious. So much more energy is naturally put into what must be done than into what it is merely expedient should be done, that the children are likely to exert their once-roused faculties to much better purpose than if their business was appointed to them for their own educational benefit. The little girl who tends the baby, or helps granny, or makes father's shirt, or learns to cook the dinner, is likely to put more mind into her work than if she were set to mark a sampler or make a doll's frock for the sake of learning to sew. And so with the boy who carries the coals for his mother, or helps his father in the workshop: he will become manly earlier and more naturally than the highborn child who sees no higher sanction for his occupations than the authority of his parents. And how dearly prized are the opportunities for book-study which can be secured! The children see what a privilege and recreation reading is to their father; and they grow up with a reverence and love for that great resource. The hope and expectation carry them through the tedious work of the alphabet and pothooks. And as they grow up, they are admitted to the magnificent privilege of fireside intercourse with the holy Milton, and the glorious Shakspeare, and many a sage whose best thoughts may become their ideas of every day. They thus obtain that activity and enlargement of mind which render all employments and all events educational. The powers, once roused and set to work, find occupation and material in every event of life. Everything serves—the daily handicraft, intercourse with the neighbours, rumours from the world without, homely duty, books, worship, the face of the country, or the action of the town. All these incitements, all this material, are offered to the thoughtful artisan more fully and impartially than to such below and above him as are hedged in by ignorance or by aristocratic seclusion: and therein is his condition better than theirs. After having come to this conclusion, it is no small satisfaction to remember that the most favoured classes are the most numerous. So great a multitude is included in the middle classes, compared with the highborn and the degraded, that if they who have the best chance for wisdom will but use their privilege, the highest hopes for society are the most reasonable.

# CHAPTER VI.
## THE NEW COMER.

We may be perverse in our notions, and mistaken in our ways; but there are some great natural blessings which we cannot refuse. I reckon it a great natural blessing that the main events of human life are common to all, and that it is out of the power of man to spoil the privilege and pleasure of them. Birth, love, and death, are beyond the reach of man's perverseness. They come differently to the wise and the foolish, the wicked and the pure: but they come alike to the rich and the poor. The infant finds as warm a bosom in which to nestle in the cottage as in the mansion. The bride and bridegroom know the bliss of being all the world to each other as well in their Sunday walk in the fields as in the park of a royal castle. And when the mourners stand within the enclosure where "rich and poor lie down together," death is the same sad and sweet mystery to all the children of mortality, whether they be elsewhere the lowly or the proud.

It may be said that the coming of the infant is not the same event to all, because some very poor people are heard to speak of it as a misfortune, and if the child dies, to rejoice that the Lord has taken it to himself. It is true that some parents are heard to speak in this way; but I believe that the difference here is not between rich and poor, but between the wise and the foolish,—the trusting and the faithless. I have a right to believe this as long as I see that the hardest-working mother can be as tender and as cheerful as any other, and that the poorest man can be as conscientious a father as the richest. If the parents have been guilty of no fault towards their unborn child; if the child be the offspring of healthful and virtuous parents; and if they are calmly resolved to do all in their power for its good,—to earn its bread, to cherish its health, to open its mind, to nourish its soul, they have as good a right to rejoice in the prospect of its birth as anybody in the world. If they steadily purpose to do their full duty by their child, they may rely upon it that all the powers of nature will help them;—that in a world wrapped round with sweet air, and blessed by sunshine, and abounding with knowledge, the human being can hardly fail of the best ends of life, if set fairly forth on his way by those who are all to him in his helpless years. A doubt of this may be pardoned in parents too hard driven by adversity, who have lost heart, and think that to be poor is to be miserable: but the doubt is not reasonable or religious; and it is likely to be fatal to the child. I need not consider it further: for I write for those who have a high purpose and a high hope in rearing children. Those who despond are unfit for the charge, and are not likely to enter into any consultation about it.

To all who have this high purpose and hope, how interesting and how holy is this expectation of the birth of a human being! The mother is happy, and can wait. The father thinks the time long till he can take his infant in his arms, and lavish his love upon it. If there are already children, they are or should be made, happy by some promise of the new blessing to come. A serious hope it should be made to them, however joyful: a hope to be spoken of only in private seasons of confidence, when parents and children speak to each other of what they feel most deeply,—by the bedsides of the little ones at night, or in the quietest time of the Sunday holiday. A serious hope it should be to all parties; for they should bring into the consideration the duties of labour and self-denial which lie before them, and the seasons of anxiety which they must undergo. Before the parents lie sleepless nights, after days of hard work,—hours and hours of that weary suffering which arises from the wailing of a sick infant: and before the entire household the duty of those self-restraints which are ever due from the stronger to the weaker. Amidst the anticipated joys of an infant's presence, these things are not to be forgotten.

When the child is born, what an event is it in the education of the whole household! According to the use made of it is it a pure blessing, or a cause of pain and sin to some concerned. If it be the first child, there is danger lest it be too engrossing to the young mother. I believe it happens oftener than anybody knows, that the first conjugal discontents follow on the birth of the first child. The young mother trusts too much to her husband's interest in her new treasure being equal to her own;—a thing which the constitution of man's nature, and the arrangements of his business, render impossible. He will love his infant dearly, and sacrifice much for it if he remains, as he ought, his wife's first object. But if she neglects his comfort to indulge in fondling her infant, she is doing wrong to both. If her husband no longer finds, on his return from his business, a clean and quiet fireside, and a wife eager to welcome him, but a litter of baby-things, and a wife too busy up-stairs to come down, or too much engaged with her infant to talk with him and make him comfortable, there is a mischief done which can never be repaired.

And if this infant be not the first, there is another person to be no less carefully considered,—the next youngest. I was early struck by hearing the mother of a large family say, that her pet was always the youngest but one; it was so hard to cease to be the baby! Little children are as jealous of affection as the most enraptured lover; and they are too young to have learned to control their passions, and to be reasonable. A more miserable being can hardly exist than a little creature who, having been accustomed to the tenderness always lavished on the baby,—having spent almost its whole life in its mother's arms, and been the first to be greeted on its father's entrance, finds itself bid to sit on its little stool, or turned over to the maid, or to rough brothers and sisters to be taken care of, while everybody gathers round the baby, to admire and love it. Angry and jealous feelings may grow into dreadful passions in that little breast, if great care be not taken to smooth over the rough passage from babyhood to childhood. If the mother would have this child love and not hate the baby, if she would have peace and not tempest reign in the little heart, she will be very watchful. She will have her eye on the little creature, and call it to help her to take care of the baby. She will keep it at her knee, and show it, with many a tender kiss between, how to make baby smile, how to warm baby's feet; will let it taste whether baby's food be nice, and then peep into the cradle, to see whether baby be asleep. And when baby is asleep, the mother will open her arms to the little helper, and fondle it as of old, and let it be all in all to her, as it used to be. This is a great piece of education to them both, and a lesson in justice to all who stand by.

The addition of a child to the family circle is an event too solemn to be deformed by any falsehood. But few parents have the courage to be truthful with their children as to how the infant comes; a question which their natural curiosity always prompts. The deceptions usually practised are altogether to be reprobated. It is an abominable practice to tell children that the doctor brought the baby, and the like. It is abominable as a lie: and it is worse than useless. Any intelligent child will go on to ask,—or if not to ask, to ponder with excited imagination,—where the doctor found it, and so on; and its attention will be piqued, and its mind injuriously set to work, where a few serious words of simple but carefully expressed truth, would have satisfied it entirely. The child must, sooner or later, awaken to an understanding of the subject; and it is no more difficult to impress him with a sense of decency about this, than about other things, that a well trained child never speaks of, but to its mother in private. The natural question once truthfully answered, the little mind is at rest, and free for the much stronger interests which are passing before its eyes.

The first month of an infant's life is usually a season of great moral enjoyment to the household. Everybody is disposed to bear and to do everything cheerfully for the sake of the new blessing. The father does not mind the dis comforts of the time of his wife's absence from the table and the fireside, and makes himself by turns the nurse and the playfellow, to carry the children well through it. If Granny be there, and not able to do much in the house, she gathers the little ones about her chair, and tells them longer stories than ever before, to keep them quiet. The children try with all their might to be quiet; and even the little two-year-old one struggles not to cry for company when baby cries, and learns a lesson in self-restraint. They look with respect on the maid or the nurse when they find that she has been up in the night, tending mother and baby, and that she looks as cheerful in the morning as if she had had good rest. And when they are permitted to study the baby, and to see how it jerks its little limbs about, and does not see anything they want it to see, and takes no notice of anything they say to it; and when they hear that their great strong father, so wise and so clever about his business, was once just such a helpless little creature as this, they learn to reverence this feeble infant, and one another, and themselves, and their hearts are very full of feelings which they cannot speak. I well remember that the strongest feelings I ever entertained towards any human being were towards a sister born when I was nine years old. I doubt whether any event in my life ever exerted so strong an educational influence over me as her birth. The emotions excited in me were overwhelming for above two years; and I recal them as vividly as ever now when I see her with a child of her own in her arms. I threw myself on my knees many times in a day, to thank God that he permitted me to see the growth of a human being from the beginning. I leaped from my bed gaily every morning as this thought beamed upon me with the morning light. I learnt all my lessons without missing a word for many months, that I might be worthy to watch her in the nursery during my play-hours. I used to sit on a stool opposite to her as she was asleep, with a Bible on my knees, trying to make out how a creature like this might rise "from strength to strength," till it became like Christ. My great pain was, (and it was truly at times a despair,) to think what a work lay before this thoughtless little being. I could not see how she was to learn to walk with such soft and pretty limbs: but the talking was the despair. I fancied that she would have to learn every word separately, as I learned my French vocabulary; and I looked at the big Johnson's Dictionary till I could not bear to think about it. If I, at nine years old, found it so hard to learn through a small book like that Vocabulary, what would it be to her to begin at two years old such a big one as that! Many a time I feared that she never could possibly learn to speak. And when I thought of all the trees and plants, and all the stars, and all the human faces she must learn, to say nothing of lessons,—I was dreadfully oppressed, and almost wished she had never been born. Then followed the relief of finding that walking came of itself—step by step; and then, that talking came of itself—word by word at first, and then many new words in a day. Never did I feel a relief like this, when the dread of this mighty task was changed into amusement at her funny use of words, and droll mistakes about them. This taught me the lesson, never since forgotten, that a way always lies open before us, for all that it is necessary for us to do, however impossible and terrible it may appear beforehand. I felt that if an infant could learn to speak, nothing is to be despaired of from human powers, exerted according to Nature's laws. Then followed the anguish of her childish illnesses—the misery of her wailing after vaccination, when I could neither bear to stay in the nursery nor to keep away from her; and the terror of the back-stairs, and of her falls, when she found her feet; and the joy of her glee when she first knew the sunshine, and the flowers, and the opening spring; and the shame if she did anything rude, and the glory when she did anything right and sweet. The early life of that child was to me a long course of intense emotions which, I am certain, have constituted the most important part of my education. I speak openly of them here, because I am bound to tell the best I know about Household Education; and on that, as on most subjects, the best we have to tell is our own experience. And I tell it the more readily because I am certain that my parents had scarcely any idea of the passions and emotions that were working within me, through my own unconsciousness of them at the time, and the natural modesty which makes children conceal the strongest and deepest of their feelings: and it may be well to give parents a hint that more is passing in the hearts of their children, on occasion of the gift of a new soul to the family circle, than the ingenuous mind can recognise for itself, or knows how to confide.

# CHAPTER VII.

## CARE OF THE FRAME.

We have seen something of the influence of the infant upon others: now let us see what others can do for it.

Here is a little creature containing within itself the germs of all those powers which have before been described; but with all these powers in so feeble a state that months and years of nourishing and cherishing under the influences of Nature are necessary to give it the use of its own powers. What its parents can do for it, and all that they can do for it, is to take care that it has the full advantage of the influences of Nature. This is their task. They cannot get beyond it, and they ought not to fall short of it.

Nature requires and provides that the tender frame should be nourished with food, air, warmth and light, sleep and exercise. All these being given to it, the soft bones will grow hard, the weak muscles will grow firm; the eye will become strong to see, and the ear to hear, and the different portions of the brain to feel, and apprehend, and think; and to form purposes, and to cause action, till the helpless infant becomes a self-acting child, and is on the way to become a rational man. What the parents have to do is to take care that the babe has the best of food, air, warmth, and light, sleep and exercise.

First, of food. About this there is no possible doubt. The mother's milk is the best of food. What the mother has to look to is that her milk is of the best. She must preserve her own health by wholesome diet, air, and exercise, and by keeping a gentle and cheerful temper. Many a babe has had convulsions after being suckled by a nurse who had had a great fright, or had been in a great passion: and a mother who has an irritable or anxious temper, who flushes or trembles with anger, or has her heart in her throat from fear of this or that, will not find her child thrive upon her milk, but will have much to suffer from its illness or its fretfulness. She must try, however busy she may be, to give it its food pretty regularly, that its stomach may not be overloaded nor long empty or craving. An infant does not refuse food when it has had enough, as grown people can do. It will stop crying and suck, when its crying is from some other cause than hunger: and it will afterwards cry all the more if an overloaded stomach is added to the other evil, whatever it may be. Of the contrary mischief—leaving a babe too long hungry—there is no need to say anything. And when the weaning time comes, it is plain that the food should be at first as like as possible to that which is given up; thin, smooth, moderately warm, fresh, and sweet, and given as leisurely as the mother's milk is drawn. It is well known that milk contains, more curiously than any other article of food, whatever is necessary for nourishing all the parts of the human body. It contains that which goes to form and strengthen the bones, and that which goes to make and enrich the blood—thereby causing the soft bones of the babe to grow stiff and strong, and its heart to beat healthily, and its lungs to play vigorously, and its muscles to thicken and become firm. While all this is going on well, and the child shows no need of other food, there is nothing but mischief to be looked for from giving it a variety for which it is not prepared. Milk, flour and water are its natural food while it has no teeth to eat meat with, and vegetables turn sour on its stomach. As for giving it a bit or sip of what grown persons are eating and drinking—that is a practice too ignorant to need to be mentioned here.

Next comes air. Here, as usual, we have to consult Nature. There is an ingredient in the air which is as necessary to support human breathing as to feed the flame of a candle. Where there is too little of it, the flame of a candle burns dim; and where it is not freely supplied to a human frame, it languishes, and pines and sickens. A constant supply of pure air there must therefore be. If the house is close, if the room is too long shut up, with people in it who are using up that ingredient of the air, they will all, and especially the babe, languish and pine and sicken. Every morning, therefore, and during the day, there must be plenty of fresh air let in to replace that which has been spoiled by breathing; and in fine weather, the babe should be carried into the open air every day. But Nature also points out that we must avoid extremes in giving the child air, as well as food. We see sometimes how a babe grows black in the face if carried with its face to the wind, or whisked down stairs in a draught. Its lungs are small and tender, like the rest of it, and can bear even fresh air only when moderately given. By a little care in turning its face away from the wind, or lightly covering its head, a child may be saved from being half strangled by a breeze out of doors; while care will, of course, be taken within doors to keep it out of the direct draught from door or window.

As for light—we do not yet know so much as we ought about the relation between light and the human frame. I believe some curious secrets remain to be discovered about that. But we do know this much—that people who live in dark places, prisoners in dungeons, and very poor people in cellars, and savages in caves who do not go abroad much, are not only less healthy than others, but have peculiar diseases which are distinctly traceable to deficiency of light. My own conviction is that we grown people can hardly have too much light in our houses; and that we are, somehow or other, alive almost in proportion to the sunshine we live in. But we must observe, at the same time, the difference which Nature makes between the infant and adults. The infant's eyes are weak, and its brain tender; so that, while there is plenty of light about its body, we must take care that there is not too much directly before its eyes. If held opposite a strong sunshine, it will squint if it does not cry, or by some means show that the light is too much for its tender brain.

As to warmth—everybody knows that a babe cannot have that constant warmth which is kept up in older persons by constant activity. Its little feet require frequent warm handling; and its lips often look blue when everybody else in the room is warm enough. By gentle chafing and warming it must be kept comfortable during the day, without being shut up in a hot room, or scorched before the fire. As for the night—its warmth should be secured by sufficient clothing, in a little bed of its own, as early as possible, rather than by lying with its mother, which is far too common a practice. It may be necessary, in extremely cold weather, to take the child into bed for warmth; but even then, the mother should not sleep till she has put it back, warm and well covered, into its own bed. I need say nothing of the horror we feel when, every now and then, we hear of a miserable mother whose child has been overlaid. That accident happens oftener than many people know of. But, besides that danger, the practice is a bad one. The child breathes air already breathed; it soaks in the perspiration of its mother. If its state is healthful, its natural sleep will keep it warm, supposing its bedding to be sufficient; while it is likely to be too hot, and not to breathe healthfully, if laid close by another person. In all seasons, its clothing should be loose enough to allow of a free play of its limbs, and of all the movements within its body—the beating of the heart, the heaving of the lungs, and the rolling of the bowels, to go on quite naturally. By careful management, an infant may be kept in a state of natural warmth, night and day, through winter and summer; as every sensible mother knows.

The little frame must be exercised. Every human function depends on exercise for its growth and perfection. A person who lives almost in the dark has little use of his eyes when he comes into the light; an arm hung in a sling becomes weak, and at last useless; a talent for arithmetic or music becomes feebler continually from disuse. To make the most therefore of the frame of a human being, it must be exercised—some of its powers from the beginning, and all in their natural order. We must take care, however, to observe what this natural order is, or, judging by our present selves, we may attempt too much. We must remember that the infant has to begin from the beginning, and that its primary organs—the heart, lungs, and brain—have to become accustomed to moderate exercise before anything further should be attempted. At first, it is quite enough for the infant to be taken up and laid down, washed and dressed, and carried about a little on the arm. When the proper time comes, it will kick and crow, and reach and handle, and look and listen. Its very crying, if only what is natural to express its wants, is a good exercise of those parts intended to be used afterwards in speaking and making childish noises. Poor Laura Bridgman, the American girl, who early lost both eyes and the inner parts of the ears, and cannot hear, see, smell, or taste, and whose mind is yet developed by means of the sense of touch, said a thing (said it by finger language) which appears to me very touching and very instructive. Not being able to speak, she was formerly apt to use the organs of speech in making odd noises, disagreeable to people about her. When told of this, and encouraged to try to be silent, she asked—"Why, then, has God given me so much voice?" Her guardians took the hint, and gave her a place to play in for some time every day, where she can make as much noise as she likes—hearing none of it herself, but enjoying the exercise to her organs of sound. What Laura does now, an infant does by squalling, and children do by shouting and vociferating at their play. Their parents, it must be remembered, are talking for many hours while they are asleep.

Other exercises follow in their natural course—the rolling and tumbling about on a thickly wadded quilt on the floor (saving the busy mother's time, while teaching the child the use of its limbs)—feeling its feet on the lap, and learning to step, scrambling up and down by the leg of the table, pulling and throwing things about, imitating sounds, till speech is attained—these are the exercises which nature directs, and under which the powers grow till the mother can see in her plaything the sailor who may one day rock at the mast-head, or the stout labourer who may trench the soil, or the gardener who will name a thousand plants at a glance, or the teacher who will bring out and train a hundred human intellects. What she has to look to is that the powers of her child are all remembered and considered, and exercised only in due degree and natural order.

After exercise comes sleep. If all else go well, this will too. If the child digest well, be warm, sufficiently fatigued and not too much—in short, if it be comfortable in body, it will sleep at proper times. One of the earliest pieces of education—of training—is to induce a babe to sleep regularly, and without the coaxing which consumes so much of the mother's time, and encourages so much waywardness on the part of the child. If a healthy child be early accustomed to a bed of its own, and if it is laid down at a sleepy moment, while the room is quiet, it will soon get into a habit of sleeping when laid down regularly, in warmth and stillness, after being well washed and satisfied with food. The process is natural; and it would happen easily enough if our ways did not interfere with Nature. By a little care, a child may be attended to in the night without fully awakening it. By watching for its stirring, veiling the light, being silent and quick, the little creature may be on its pillow again without having quite waked up—to its own and its mother's great advantage.

Cleanliness is the removal of all that is unwholesome. Nature has made health dependent upon this, in the case of human beings of every age: and the more eminently, the younger they are. One great condition of an infant's welfare is the removal of all discharges whatever, by careful cleansing of the delicate skin in every crease and corner, every day; and of all clothing as soon as soiled. The perpetual washing of an infant's bibs, &c., is a great trouble to a busy mother; but less than to have the child ill from the smell of a sour pinafore, or from wet underclothes, or from a cap that holds the perspiration of a week's nights and days. It is a thing which must be done—the keeping all pure and sweet about the body of the little creature that cannot help itself; and its look of welfare amply repays the trouble all the while.

Such are the offices to be rendered to the new-born infant. They consist in allowing Nature scope for her higher offices. By their faithful discharge, the human being is prepared to become in due season all that he is made capable of being—which may prove to be something higher than we are at present aware of.

# CHAPTER VIII.
## CARE OF THE POWERS:—WILL.

While the bodily powers of the infant are nourished and preserved by observing Nature, as pointed out in the last chapter, the powers of the mind are growing from day to day. When an infant has once been pleased with the glitter of the sun upon the brass warming-pan, or with the sound of a rattle, it will kick and shake its little arms, and look eager, the next time it sees the rattle and the warming-pan. And having once remembered, it will remember more every day. Every day it will give signs of Hope and Desire. Will shows itself very early. Fear has to be guarded against, and Love to be cherished, from the first days that mind appears. It is the highest possible privilege to the child if the parents know how to exercise its power of Conscience soon enough, so as to make it sweet and natural to the young creature to do right from its earliest days. Let us see how these things may be.

How strong is the Will of even a very young infant! How the little creature, if let alone, will labour and strive after anything it has set its mind upon! How it cries and struggles to get the moon; and tumbles about the floor, as soon as it can sprawl, to accomplish any wish! And, if ill-trained, how pertinaciously it will refuse to do anything it ought! How completely may the wills of a whole party of grown people be set at nought by the self-will of a baby whose powers are allowed to run riot! It is exceedingly easy to mismanage such cases, as we all see every day: but it is also very easy to render this early power of Will a great blessing.

The commonest mistake is to indulge the child's self-will, as the easiest course at the moment. Immediate peace and quiet are sought by giving the child whatever it clamours for, and letting it do whatever it likes in its own way. We need not waste words on this tremendous mistake. Everybody knows what a spoiled child is; and nobody pretends to stand up for the method of its education. I think quite as ill of the opposite mistake—of the method which goes by the name of breaking the child's will; a method adopted by some really conscientious parents because they think religion requires it. When I was in America, I knew a gentleman who thought it his first duty to break the wills of his children; and he set about it zealously and early. He was a clergyman, and the President of an University: the study of his life had been the nature and training of the human mind: and the following is the way he chose—misled by a false and cruel religion of Fear—to subdue and destroy the great faculty of Will. An infant of (I think) about eleven months old was to be weaned. A piece of bread was offered to the babe; and the babe turned away from it. Its father said that it was necessary to break down the rebellious will of every child for once; that if done early enough, once would suffice; and that it would be right and kind to take this early occasion in the instance of this child. The child was therefore to be compelled to eat the bread. A dressmaker in the house saw the process go on through the whole day; and became so dreadfully interested that she could not go away at night till the matter was finished. Of course, the bit of bread became more and more the subject of disgust, and then of terror to the infant, the more it was forced upon its attention. Hours of crying, shrieking and moaning were followed by its being shut up in a closet. It was brought out by candlelight—stretched helpless across the nurse's arms, its voice lost, its eyes sunk and staring, its muscles shrunk, its appearance that of a dying child. It was now near midnight. The bit of bread was thrust into the powerless hand; no resistance was offered by the unconscious sufferer; and the victory over the evil powers of the flesh and the devil was declared to be gained. The dressmaker went home, bursting with grief and indignation, and told the story: and when the President went abroad the next morning, he found the red brick walls of the university covered with chalk portraits of himself holding up a bit of bread before his babe. The affair made so much noise that he was, after some time, compelled to publish a justification of himself. This justification amounted to what was well understood throughout; that he conscientiously believed it his duty to take an early opportunity to break the child's will, for its own sake. There remained for his readers the old wonder where he could find in the book of Glad Tidings so cruel a contradiction of that law of love which stands written on every parent's heart.

How much easier is the true and natural method for controlling the young Will! Nature points out that the true method is to control the Will, not by another person's Will, but by the other faculties of the child itself. When the child wills what is right and innocent, let the faculty work freely. When it wills what is wrong and hurtful, appeal to other faculties, and let this one sleep; excite the child's attention; engage its memory, or its hope, or its affection. If the infant is bent on having something that it ought not, put the forbidden object out of sight, and amuse the child with something else. Avoid both indulgence and opposition, and a habit of docility will be formed by the time the child becomes capable of deliberate self-control. This natural method being followed, it is curious to see how early the power of self-control may be attained. I watched one case of a child endowed with a strong Will who, well trained, had great power of self-government before she could speak plain. She was tenderly reared, and indulged in her wishes whenever they were reasonable, and cheerfully amused and helped whenever her desires were disappointed. One day I had just begun to show her a bright new red pocket-book full of pictures when she was called to her dinner. She did not want her dinner, and begged to see the pocket-book; begged it once—twice—and was about to beg it a third time, when I ventured to put to the proof her power of self-denial. I put the case before her as it appeared to me, fairly saying that I could not show her the pocket-book till five in the afternoon. Showing her what I thought the right of the matter, I asked her whether she would now go to her dinner. She stood, with the pocket-book in her hand, for some seconds in deep thought; then looked up at me with a bright face, said graciously "I will;" put the gay plaything into my lap, and ran off to her dinner. The looking forward till five o'clock and the pleasure of that hour fixed the effort in her mind, and made the next easier. It is clear that a child early subject to oppression and opposition in matters of the Will could not arrive thus betimes and naturally at self-government like this, but must have many perverse and painful feelings to struggle with, in addition to the necessary conflict with himself.

A parent who duly appreciates the great work that every human being has to do in attaining self-government, will assist the process from the very first, by the two great means in his power—by the aid of Habit, and of a government of love instead of fear. It is really due to the feebleness of a child to give it the aid and support of habit in what it has to do and avoid. By regularity in the acts of its little life, in its sleeping and feeding, and walking and times of play, a world of conflict and wilfulness is avoided, and the will is quietly trained, day by day, to submission to circumstances; life goes on with the least possible wear and tear; and a continually strengthening power is obtained over all the faculties. Among the children entering upon school life, and men and women upon any sphere of duty whatever, a great difference as to efficiency will be found between those who always have to bring their Will to bear expressly on the business of the time, unaided by habit, and those whose lives and powers have been, as one may say, economised by their having lived under that discipline of time and circumstance which is the gentle and natural education of the human Will. It is true, this mechanical kind of discipline can never be more than auxiliary. It can never stand in the place of the deep internal principle by which alone the mightiest movements of the human will are actuated. It can only husband a man's powers for his ordinary duties, and not of itself prepare him for the great crises of life. It can only aid him in his everyday course, and not strengthen him, when the agonising hour comes, to surrender love, and hope, and peace, at the call of duty, or to encounter outrage and death for truth's sake. But we are now considering the education of the infant man; man at that stage when our chief concern is with whatever is auxiliary to that great aim of perfection which lies far in the future.

Above all things it is important that the parental administration should be one of love and not of fear. There can be no healthful growth of the Will under the restraints of fear. The fact is, the Will is not trained at all in any frightened person.

The actions may be conformed to the Will of the tyrant; but the Will is running riot in secret all the time—unless, indeed, it be entirely crushed. But how vigorously it grows under a government of love! Look at the difference between a slave-owner, whose people are driven by the lash, and an employer whose people are ready to live and die for him: how languidly and shabbily is the work done in the first case, and how heartily and efficiently in the last! And it is with the young child as with the grown man. A child who lives in the fear of punishment has half its faculties absorbed by that fear, and becomes a feeble little creature, incapable of governing itself; while a mere babe who is cheered and led on in its good efforts by smiles of love and tones of tenderness becomes strong to govern its passions, and to brush away its tears; and patient to bear pain; and brave to overcome difficulty; becomes blessed, in short, with a healthful and virtuous Will. I know nothing more touching than the efforts of self-government of which little children are capable, when the best parts of their nature are growing vigorously under the light and warmth of parental love. Mrs. Wesley might pride herself on so breaking the wills of her children by fear as that the youngest in arms learned immediately "to cry softly;" but there was every danger that the early cowed Will would sooner or later start up in desperate rebellion, and claim a freedom which it would be wholly unable to manage. How much safer, and how infinitely more beautiful is the self-control of the little creature who stifles his sobs of pain because his mother's pitying eye is upon him in tender sorrow! or that of the babe who abstains from play, and sits quietly on the floor because somebody is ill; or that of a little hero who will ask for physic if he feels himself ill, or for punishment if he knows himself wrong, out of confidence in the tender justice of the rule under which he lives! I have known a very young child slip over to the cold side of the bed on a winter's night, that a grown-up sister might find a warm one. I have known a boy in petticoats offer his precious new humming-top to a beggar child. I have known a little girl submit spontaneously to hours of irksome restraint and disagreeable employment merely because it was right. Such Wills as these—so strong and yet so humble, so patient and so dignified—were never impaired by fear, but flourished thus under the influence of love, with its sweet incitements and holy supports.

# CHAPTER IX.

## CARE OF THE POWERS:—HOPE.

We have seen what power of Will a child has. But the Will itself is put in action by Hope and Fear.

What is stronger in an infant than its capacity for Hope and Fear? In its earliest and most unconscious stages of emotion, how its little limbs quiver, and its countenance lights up at the prospect of its food! and how it turns away its face, or wrinkles it up into a cry, at the sight of a strange countenance, or unusual appearance of dress or place! And what stronger hint can a parent have than this to look forward to what this hope and fear may grow to?

This great power of Hope must determine the leading features of the character of the man or woman; determine them for good or evil according to the training of the power from this day forward. Shall the man continue a child, or sink into the brute by his objects of hope continuing to be what they are now—food or drink? Shall his frame be always put into commotion by the prospect of pleasant bodily sensations from eating and drinking, and other animal gratifications? Or, when the child arrives at hoping for his mother's smile and his father's praise, shall he stop there, and live for admiration; admiration of his person and dress, his activity, or his cleverness? Shall the gratification of his vanity be the chief interest of his life? Or shall it be ambition? Shall his perpetual hope be of a higher sort of praise—praise from so large a number as shall give him power over other men, and cause his name to be known beyond his connexions, and his native place, and his country and his age? All this is very low and very small; too little for the requirements of his nature, too little for the peace of his mind and the happiness of his heart. Shall not rather this faculty of hope be nourished up into Faith?—faith which includes at once the fulness of virtuous power and the peace which the world can neither give nor take away. A being in whom the early faculty of Hope has been matured into a steady power of Faith is of the highest and happiest order of men, because the objects of his hope are unchanging and ever-lasting, and they keep all his best powers in strenuous action and in full health and strength. When the mother sees her infant in an ecstacy of hope, first at the food making ready for him, and next at the gay flower within his reach, and afterwards at the flattery of visitors, she should remember that here is the faculty which may hereafter lead and sustain him through days of hunger and nights of watching, or years of toilsome obscurity, or scenes of the unthinking world's scorn, calm and peaceful in the furtherance of the truth of God and the welfare of Man. And if her tender heart shrinks from the anticipation of privation and contempt such as have too often hitherto attended a life of faith, let her remember that in the midst of the most prosperous life there can be no peace but in proportion to the power of faith; and that therefore in training up this faculty of Hope to its highest exercise she is providing most substantially for his happiness, be his lot otherwise what it may.

How is this faculty to be trained?—

First, it must be cherished. Some well-meaning parents repress and even extinguish it, from the notion that this is the way to teach humility and self-denial. The consequence is that they break the mainspring of action in the child's mind, and everything comes to a stand. It is difficult to weaken the power of hope in a human being, and harder still to break it down; but when the thing is done, what sadder spectacle can be seen? Of all moving sights of woe, the most mournful is that of a hopeless child. A single glance at its listless limbs, its dull eye, its languid movements, shows the mischief that has been done. The child is utterly unreliable; a mere burden upon the world. He has no truth, no love, no industry, no intellectual power in him; and if he has any conscience, it is the mere remains,—enough to trouble him, without doing him any good. This is an extreme case, and I trust a rare one. But cases of repressed hope are much more common than they should be. There are too many children who are baulked of their mother's sympathy because she is busy or fretful, or of their father's, because he is stern. Too many little hearts are made to swell in silence because they cannot get justice, or to burn under the suspicion that their aspirations are despised. After this, what can they do? At best, they carry their confidence elsewhere, and make their chief interests away from home: and it is too probable that they will give up their plans and aspirations, and sink down to lower hopes. A boy who aspires to discover the North Pole, or to write a book which will teach the world something greater than it ever knew before, will presently sink down to be greedy after lollypops: and a girl who means to try whether a woman cannot be as good as Jesus Christ, may presently be discouraged down to the point of reckoning on Sunday because she is to have a new ribbon on her bonnet. In the case of every human being, Hope is to be cherished from first to last; not the hope of the particular thing that the child has set its mind on, unless the thing itself be good; but the hopeful mood of mind. The busiest mother can have nothing to do so important as satisfying her child's heart by a word or look of sympathy: and the most anxious father can have nothing so grave to occupy him as the peril he puts his child into by plunging him into undeserved fear and disappointment.

Hope is to be cherished without ceasing. But the objects of hope must first be varied and then exalted, that the faculty may be led on from strength to strength, till it is able to fix its aims for itself. To the hope of good eating and drinking must succeed that of clutching gay colours, of hearing mother sing, of having play with father when he comes home; then of having a kitten or a doll to take care of; then of parents' praise for lessons or other work well done; then of self-satisfaction for bad habits cured: then there may be a great spring forward to thoughts of glory;—the glory of being a great sailor, or magistrate, or author, or martyr: and at length, the hope of doing great things for the good of mankind, and of becoming a perfect man. As for times and opportunities of cherishing and exalting hope—every hour is the right time, and every day affords the opportunity. What is needed, is that the parents should have the aim fixed in their hearts; and then their minds, and that of the child, will work towards it as by an instinct. By natural impulse the mother's hand will bring the gay flower, and the kitten or the doll before the child's notice, if it becomes greedy about its food. By natural impulse she will sing its favourite song, or beg play for it of its father after some little virtuous effort of the child's; in natural course, all things in human life, great and small, will present themselves in their heroic aspect to the minds of the parents, and be thus represented to the mind of the child, if once the idea of the future man be firmly associated with that of moral nobleness. If they have in them faith enough steadily to desire for him this moral nobleness above all things, there can be no fear but that their aspiration will communicate itself to him; and his faculty of Hope will ripen into a power of Faith.

I have said nothing of a hope of reward as among the objects of childhood. This is because I think rewards and punishments seldom or never necessary in household education, while they certainly bring great mischief after them. In some cases of bad habit, and in a very early stage of education, they may be desirable, here and there; but as a system, I think rewards and punishments bad. In the case of a very young child who has fallen into a habit of crying at bedtime, or at any particular time of day, or in that of a thoughtless, untidy child, where the object is to impress its memory, or to establish a strong association with time or place, it may be useful to connect some expectation of pain or pleasure with particular seasons or acts, so as to make the infant remember the occasion for self-government, and rouse its will to do right; but this should be only where the association of selfish pleasure or pain is likely to die out with the bad habit, and never where such selfish pleasure or pain can be associated with great permanent ideas and moral feelings. A careless child may be allowed to earn a reward for punctuality at meals, and for putting playthings and dress in their proper place when done with, and for personal neatness, during a specified time; and perhaps for the diligent learning of irksome tasks: and there may be some punishment, declared and agreed upon before hand, and steadily inflicted, for any disagreeable personal habit, or any other external instance of habitual thoughtlessness. But the greater moral aims of the parent are too sacred to be mixed up with the direct personal interests of the child. A child will hardly be nobly truthful who dreads being whipped for a lie; and benevolence will be spoiled in its young beginnings, if any pleasure beyond itself is looked for in its early exercise. A child who has broken a plate, or gone astray for pleasure when sent on an errand, must want confidence in his parents, and be more or less cowardly if he denies the offence; and he will not have more truth or courage on the next occasion for being whipped now. What he needs is to be made wiser about the blessedness of truth and the horrors of falsehood, and more brave about the pain of rebuke: and the whipping will not make him either the one or the other. I remember being fond of a book in my childhood which yet revolted me in one part. It told of the children of a great family in France, who heard of the poverty of a woman about to lie in, and who bought and made clothes for herself and her infant. Their mother and grandmother made a sort of festival of the giving of these clothes. The children rode in procession on asses, carrying their gifts. One tied her bundle with blue ribbon, and another with pink; and the whole village came out to see, when they alighted at the poor woman's door. I used to blush with indignation over this story; indignation on the poor woman's account, that her pauperism was so exposed; and on that of the children, that they were not allowed the pure pleasure of helping a neighbour, without being applauded at home and by a whole village for what it gave them nothing but satisfaction to do. I am strongly of opinion that when we duly understand and estimate man, there will be no reward or punishment at all; that human beings will be so trained as to find their pleasure and pain in the gratification or the abuse of their own highest faculties; and that in those days (however far off they may be) there will be no treadwheels, no hulks, no gibbets; and no prize-giving, except for feats of skill or activity. And meantime, I feel perfectly sure that children under home-training may be led to find such gratification in the exercise of their higher intellectual and moral faculties, as to feel the abuse of them more painful than any punishment, and their action more pleasurable than any reward. When we read of a Christian in the early ages who was brought into the amphitheatre, and given the choice whether he would declare Jupiter to be the supreme God, and enjoy life and comfort, or avow himself a Christian, and be torn to pieces by wild beasts the next minute, we feel that he could not say he believed Jupiter to be God. Well: convince any child as fully as this of the truth, and of his absolute need of fidelity to it, and he can no more endure lapse from it than the Christian could endure to declare Jupiter to be God. As the inveterate drunkard must gratify his propensity to drink, at the cost of any amount of personal and domestic misery; and as the miser must go on adding to his stores of gold, even though he starves himself into disease and death, so the upright man must satisfy his conscience through every extremity; and no penalty can deter the benevolent man from devoting all he has to give—his money, his time, and his life—to the relief of suffering. On such as these—the upright and the devoted—every appeal to their lower faculties is lost; and as for their hope and fear—they have passed into something higher. With them "perfect love has cast out fear;" and hope has grown up into Faith; and this faith being to them "the substance of things hoped for, the evidence of things not seen," it must be more to them than any of the passing pains and pleasures of life. Exalted as these beings are, they are of the same make as the infant on its mother's lap: and each is destined to derive his highest gratification from the exercise of the noblest faculties of his nature. If parents did but understand and constantly remember this, they would consider well before they dared to mix up a meaner pleasure and pain with the greater, while appealing to any of the higher moral faculties of their children—if indeed they ventured upon reward and punishment at all.

# CHAPTER X.

## CARE OF THE POWERS CONTINUED:—FEAR.

There is nothing in which children differ more than in their capacity for Fear. But every child has it more or less,—or ought to have it: for nothing can be made of a human being who has never experienced it. A child who has never known any kind of fear can have no power of Imagination;—can feel no wonder, no impulse of life, no awe or veneration. Such a case probably does not exist, except in a condition of idiotcy. A child who is called fearless, and who is congratulated upon this,—who shows no shyness of strangers, who does not mind cold water, or falls, or being in the dark, who runs after animals, and plays with ugly insects, may yet cower under a starry sky, or tremble at thunder, or be impressed for life by a mysterious dream. It is for the parents to watch the degree and direction of an infant's fear, firmly assured that whatever be this degree and direction, all may end well under prudent care.

The least favourable case is that of the apathetic child. When it appears indifferent to whatever may happen to it, and shrinks from nothing, it must be as incapable of hope and enjoyment as of fear, and there must be something amiss in its health,—in its nervous system; and its health is what must be looked to first. It must be well nourished and amused; its perceptive faculties must be exercised, and every sort of activity must be encouraged. If this succeeds, and its feelings begin to show themselves, fear will come with the rest; and then its education in that respect must begin. But it must ever be carefully remembered that fear often puts on the appearance of apathy,—especially in a proud child. No creature is so intensely reserved as a proud and timid child: and the cases are few in which the parents know anything of the agonies of its little heart, the spasms of its nerves, the soul-sickness of its days, the horrors of its nights. It hides its miseries under an appearance of indifference or obstinacy, till its habitual terror impairs its health, or drives it into a temper of defiance or recklessness. I can speak with some certainty of this, from my own experience. I was as timid a child as ever was born; yet nobody knew or could know, the extent of this timidity; for though abundantly open about everything else, I was as secret as the grave about this. I had a dream at four years old which terrified me to such an excess that I cannot now recal it without a beating of the heart. I could not look up at the sky on a clear night; for I felt as if it was only just above the tree tops, and must crush me. I could not cross the yard except at a run, from a sort of feeling, with no real belief,—that a bear was after me. The horrors of my nights were inexpressible. The main terror however was a magic-lantern which we were treated with once a year, and sometimes twice. We used to talk of this exhibition as a prodigious pleasure; and I contrived to reckon on it as such:

but I never saw the white cloth, with its circle of yellow light, without being in a cold perspiration from head to foot. One of the pictures on the slides was always suppressed by my father, lest it should frighten the little ones;— a dragon's head, vomiting flames. He little thought that a girl of thirteen could be terrified by this: but when I was thirteen,—old enough to be put in charge of some children who were to see the magic lantern,—this slide was exhibited by one of my brothers among the rest. I had found it hard enough to look and laugh before; and now I turned so faint that I could not stand, but by grasping a chair. But for the intensity of my shame, I should have dropped. Much of the benefit of instruction was lost to me during all the years that I had masters: my memory failed me when they knocked at the door, and I could never ask a question, or get voice to make a remark. I could never play to my music master, or sing with a clear voice but when I was sure nobody could hear me. Under all this, my health was bad; my behaviour was dogged and provoking, and my temper became for a time insufferable. Its improvement began from the year when I first obtained some release from habitual fear. During these critical years I misled everybody about me by a habit of concealment on this one subject which I am sure I should not now have strength for under any inducement whatever. Because I climbed our apple tree, and ran along the top of a high wall, and took great leaps, and was easily won by benevolent strangers, and because I was never known to hint or own myself afraid, no one suspected that fear was at the bottom of the immoveable indifference and apparently unfeeling obstinacy by which I perplexed and annoyed everybody about me. I make these confessions willingly, in the hope that some inexperienced or busy parent may be awakened by them to observe whether the seeming apathy of a child be really from indifference, or the outward working of some hidden passion of fear.

Bold children are good and promising subjects; and it is a delightful thing to a parent's heart to see an infant fairly trying its powers against difficulties and obstacles—confronting nature in all seasons of light and darkness, of sunshine and tempest, in the face of strangers and friends alike, free and fearless. It is delightful to think how much misery and embarrassment he is spared, by his happy constitution of nerves and brain. But, while the proud parent sees in him the future discoverer or sailor, or leader among men, it must be remembered that in order to become great, in order to become truly a man at all, he must learn and endure much that can be learned and endured only through fear, and the conquest of it. That there is some fear in him is certain; and the parent must silently search it out, and train it up into that awe and modesty which are necessary to the high courage of a whole life. No man or woman can be a faithful servant of Duty, qualified to live, suffer, and die for it, who has not grown up in awe of something higher than himself—in veneration of some powers greater than he can understand; and this awe and veneration have in them a large element of fear at the beginning. What this element is, in each case, the parents must set themselves to understand. Too many think it their duty to make a child afraid, if fear does not seem to come of itself: and too many do this without thinking it their duty, from the spirit of opposition being excited in themselves, from the experience of inconvenient fearlessness in the child. I have known a tutor avow his practice of beating a bold boy till he broke two canes over him, because the boy ought to learn that he is under a power (a power of arm) greater than his own, and must, through fear of it, apply himself to his appointed business. Such inflictions make a boy reckless, or obstinate, or deceitful. And I have seen far too many instances of irritable parents who have tried to manage a high-spirited child by threats; and, the threats failing, by blows, or shutting up in the dark, or hobgoblin prophecies, which have created no real awe or obedience, but only defiance, or forced and sullen submission. This will never do. A tender parent will never have the heart to breed fear in a child, knowing that "fear hath torment." A truly loving parent will know that it would be less unkind to bruise his child's limbs, or burn its flesh, than to plant torturing feelings in his mind. The most effectual way, for all purposes, is to discover the fear that is already there, in order to relieve him from it, by changing this weakness into a source of strength and comfort. What is it—this fear that lies hidden in him? A boy who is not afraid of the dark, or of a bull, or of a ghost, may tremble at the sight of a drunken man, or at the hearing of an oath. A girl who is not afraid of a spider or a toad, nor of thieves, nor of climbing ladders, may tremble at the moaning of the wind in the chimney, or at a frown from her mother, or at entering a sick chamber. Whatever be the fear, let the parents watch, carefully but silently, till they have found it out: and, having found it out, let them lead on the child to conquest, both by reason and by bringing such courage as he has to bear on the weak point. In any case, whether of a bold or a timid child, the only completely effectual training comes from the parents' example. If the every day life of the parents shows that they dread nothing but doing wrong, for either themselves or their children, the fears of the most timid and of the boldest will alike take this direction, sooner or later: and the courage of both will, with more or less delay, become adequate to bear and do anything for conscience' sake. If it be the clear rule and habit of an entire household to dread and detest only one thing, the fear and dislike of every mind in the household will become concentred upon that one thing, and every heart will become stout to avoid and repel it. And if the one dreaded thing be sin, it is well; for the courage of each and all will be perpetually reinforced by the whole strength of the best faculties of every mind.

As for the case of the timid child,—let not the parent be disheartened, for the noblest courage of man or woman has often grown out of the excessive fears of the child. It is true, the little creature is destined to undergo many a moment of agony, many an hour of misery, many a day of discouragement; but all this pain may be more than compensated for by the attainment of such a freedom and strength at last as may make it feel as if it had passed from hell to heaven. Think what it must be for a being who once scarcely dared to look round from fear of lights on the ceiling or shadows on the wall, who started at the patter of the rain, or the rustle of the birds leaving the spray, who felt suffocated by the breeze and maddened by the summer lightning, to pass free, fear less and glad through all seasons and their change,—all climes and their mysteries and dangers;—to pass exhilarated through raging seas, over glaring deserts, and among wild forests! Think what it must be for a creature who once trembled before a new voice or a grave countenance, and writhed under a laugh of ridicule, and lied, at the cost of deep mental agony, to avoid a rebuke,—think what it must be to such a creature to find itself at last free and fearless,—enjoying such calm satisfaction within as to suffer nothing from the ridicule or the blame of those who do not know his mind, and so thoroughly acquainted with the true values of things as to have no dread of sickness or poverty, or the world's opinion, because no evil that can befal him can touch his peace! Think what a noble work it will be to raise your trembling little one to such a condition as this, and you will be eager to begin the task at once, and patient and watchful to continue it from day to day.

First, how to begin. The most essential thing for a timid infant is to have an absolutely unfailing refuge in its mother. It may seem unnecessary to say this. It may appear impossible that a mother's tenderness should ever fail towards a helpless little creature who has nothing but that tenderness to look to: but alas! it is not so. I know a lady who is considered very sweet-tempered, and who usually is so—kind and hospitable, and fond of her children. Her infant under six months old was lying on her arm one day when the dessert was on the table; and the child was eager after the bright glasses and spoons, and more restless than was convenient. After several attempts to make it lie quiet, the mother slapped it—slapped it hard. This was from an emotion of disappointed vanity, from vexation that the child was not "good" before visitors. If such a thing could happen, may we not fear that other mothers may fail in tenderness,—in the middle of the night, for instance, after a toilsome day, when kept awake by the child's restlessness, or amidst the hurry of the day, when business presses, and the little creature will not take its sleep? Little do such mothers know the fatal mischief they do by impairing their child's security with them. If they did, they would undergo anything before they would let a harsh word or a sharp tone escape them, or indulge in a severe look or a hasty movement. A child's heart responds to the tones of its mother's voice like a harp to the wind; and its only hope for peace and courage is in hearing nothing but gentleness from her, and experiencing nothing but unremitting love, whatever may be its troubles elsewhere. Supposing this to be all right, the mother will feel herself from the first the depositary of its confidence;—a confidence as sacred as any other, though tacit, and about matters which may appear to all but itself and her infinitely small. Entering by sympathy into its fears, she will incessantly charm them away, till the child becomes open to reason,—and even afterwards; for the most terrible fears are precisely those which have nothing to do with reason. She will bring it acquainted with every object in the room or house, letting it handle in merry play everything which could look mysterious to its fearful eyes, and rendering it familiar with every household sound. Some of my worst fears in infancy were from lights and shadows. The lamp-lighter's torch on a winter's afternoon, as he ran along the street, used to cast a gleam, and the shadows of the window frames on the ceiling; and my blood ran cold at the sight, every day, even though I was on my father's knee, or on the rug in the middle of the circle round the fire. Nothing but compulsion could make me enter our drawing-room before breakfast on a summer morning; and if carried there by the maid, I hid my face in a chair that I might not see what was dancing on the wall. If the sun shone (as it did at that time of day,) on the glass lustres on the mantel-piece, fragments of gay colour were cast on the wall; and as they danced when the glass drops were shaken, I thought they were alive,—a sort of imps. But, as I never told any body what I felt, these fears could not be met, or charmed away; and I grew up to an age which I will not mention before I could look steadily at prismatic colours dancing on the wall. Suffice it that it was long after I had read enough of Optics to have taught any child how such colours came there. Many an infant is terrified at the shadow of a perforated night-lamp, with its round spaces of light. Many a child lives in perpetual terror of the eyes of portraits on the walls,—or of some grotesque shape in the pattern of the paper-hangings. Sometimes the terror is of the clack of the distant loom, or of the clink from the tinman's, or of the rumble of carts under a gateway, or of the creak of a water-wheel, or the gush of a mill-race. Everything is or may be terrifying to a timid infant; and it is therefore a mother's charge to familiarise it gently and playfully with everything that it can possibly notice, making sport with all sights, and inciting it to imitation of all sounds—from the drone of the pretty bee to the awful cry of the old clothes-man;—from the twitter of the sparrows on the roof to the toll of the distant church bell.

It is a matter of course that no mother will allow any ignorant person to have access to her child who will frighten it with goblin stories, or threats of the old black man. She might as well throw up her charge at once, and leave off thinking of household education altogether, as permit her child to be exposed to such maddening inhumanity as this. The instances are not few of idiotcy or death from terror so caused.

While thus preventing or scattering fears which arise from the imagination, both parents should be constantly using the little occasions which are always arising, for exercising their child's courage. The most timid children have always courage in one direction or another. While I was trembling and fainting under magic-lanterns and street cries, I could have suffered any pain and died any death without fear, the circumstances being fairly laid before me. Let the timid child be made hardy in its play by example and encouragement. Let it be cheered on to meet necessary pain without flinching,—the taking out a thorn, or pulling out a tooth. Let it early hear of real heroic deeds,—hear them spoken of with all the affectionate admiration with which we naturally speak of such acts. If a life is saved from fire or drowning, let the children hear of it as a joyful fact. Let them hear how steadily William Tell's little son stood, for his father to shoot through the apple. Let them hear how the good man who was on his way to be burnt for his religion took off his shoes, and gave them to a barefooted man who came to stare at him, saying that the poor man wanted the shoes, but he could do without them now. Let them hear of the other good man who was burnt for his religion, and who promised some friends, in danger of the same fate, that he would clasp his hands above his head in the midst of the fire, if he found the pain so bearable that he did not repent, and who did lift up his arms and join them after his hands were consumed,—so giving his friends on the hill-side comfort and strength. If any child of your acquaintance does a brave thing, or bears pain cheerfully, let your children hear of it as a good and happy thing. Above all, let them see, as I said before, all their lives long, that you fear nothing but wrong-doing,—neither tempests nor comets, nor reports of famine or fever, nor the tongues of the quarrelsome, nor any other of the accidents of life,—no pain, in short, but pain of conscience,—and the same spirit will strengthen in them. Their fear will follow the direction of yours; their courage will come in sympathy with yours; and their minds will fill more and more with thoughts of hope and heroism which must in time drive out such remaining terrors as cannot be met by fact or reason.

In this fearlessness of yours is included fearlessness for your children, as well as for yourselves. While their limbs are soft and feeble, of course you must be strength and safety to them: but when they arrive at a free use of their limbs and senses, let them fully enjoy that free use. We English are behind almost every nation in the strength and hardihood of the race of children. In America, I have seen little boys and girls perched in trees overhanging fearful precipices, and crawling about great holes in bridges, while the torrent was rushing below; and I could not learn that accidents from such practices were ever heard of. In Switzerland I have seen mere infants scrambling among the rocks after the goats,—themselves as safe as kids, from the early habit of relying on their own powers. In Egypt and Nubia I have seen five-year old boys poppling about like ducks in the rapids of the Nile, while some, not much older, were not satisfied with hauling and pushing, as our boat ascended the cataract, but swam and dived, to heave off her keel from sunken rocks. Such children are saved from danger, as much as from fear, by an early use of all the powers they have: and it would be a happy thing for many an English child if its parents were brave enough to encourage it to try how much it can do with its wonderful little body. Of this, however, we shall have to say more under another head.

# CHAPTER XI.
## CARE OF THE POWERS CONTINUED:—PATIENCE.

Some may be surprised to find Patience spoken of among the Powers of Man. They have been accustomed to consider it a passive quality, and not as involving action of the mind. They do not find it in any catalogue of the organs of the brain, and have always supposed it a mere negation of the action of those organs.

But patience is no negation. It is the vigorous and sustained action, amidst outward stillness, of some of the most powerful faculties with which the human being is endowed; and primarily of its powers of Firmness and Resistance. The man who holds up his head, quiet and serene, through a season of unavoidable poverty or undeserved disgrace, is exercising his power of Firmness as vigorously as the general who pursues his warfare without change of purpose through a long campaign; and a lame child, strong and spirited, who sits by cheerfully to see his companions leaping ditches, is or has been engaged in as keen a combat with opposing forces as a couple of pugilists. In the case of the patient, the resolution and resistance are brought to bear against invisible enemies, which are the more, and not the less, hard to conquer from their assaults being made in silence, and having to be met in the solitude of the inner being. The man patient under poverty or disgrace has to carry on an active interior conflict with his baffled hope, his grieved domestic affections, his natural love of ease and enjoyment, his mortified ambition, his shaken self-esteem, and his yearning after sympathy. And the lame child among the leapers has to contend alone with most of these mortifications, and with his stimulating animal spirits besides. Nothing can be further from passiveness than his state in his hour of trial, though he may sit without moving a muscle. He is putting down the swellings of his little heart, and taming his instincts, and rousing his will, and searching out noble supports among his highest ideas and best feelings—putting on his invisible armour as eagerly as any hero whom the trumpet calls from his rest.

Patience is no more like passiveness in its smallest exercises than in these great ones. Look at the ill-nursed passive infant,—how it hangs over its mother's shoulder, or slouches on her arm,—its eye dull, its face still, its movements slow: see how, when old enough to amuse itself, it sits on the floor by the hour together, jangling a bunch of keys, lulling itself with that noise, instead of making any of its own! Contrast with this the lively infant beginning to be trained to patience. It does not cry for its food or toy, as it used to do, but its limbs are all active, it fidgets, and it searches its mother's face for hope and encouragement not to cry. And when more advanced, how busy is its little soul while it makes no noise, and postpones its play for the sake of the baby. If it sits at watch beside the cradle, how it glances about to warn away the kitten, or puts its finger on its lips if the door opens, or watches so intently for baby's eye-lids to open as to start when it jerks its hand. If waiting for play till baby has had its meal, how it stands at its mother's knee, making folds in her gown,—see-sawing its body perhaps, and fetching deep sighs, to throw off its impatience, but speaking no word—making no complaint till baby has had its dues. And when its turn is come, baby being laid down, what a spring into the lap, what a clasp of the neck is there! while the child with the keys has to be lifted from the floor like a bag of sand.

As patience includes strong action of the mind, the vivacious child has a much better chance of becoming patient than the passive one;—so far are passiveness and patience from being alike. Patience is indeed the natural first step in that self-government which is essential to the whole purpose of human life. It is impossible to overrate the importance of this self-government; and therefore it is impossible to overrate the importance of this first step,—the training to patience. And the vivacious child is happy above the apathetic one in being fitted to enter at once upon the training from the earliest moment that the will is naturally capable of action.

And now about this training.

It must begin before the little creature is capable of voluntary effort. The mother must take its little troubles upon herself, and help it all she can, till the habit of patience is completely formed;—which will be long. She must not only comfort it in its restlessness and inability to wait, but beguile it of its impatience. She must amuse it, and turn away its attention from its grievance, or its object of desire,—never yielding what it ought not to have, and always indulging it where there is no reason for denial. In time, the infant will learn that it can wait, and in what cases it must wait; and from that time, its work of self-control begins. I have before my mind's eye a little child of sensitive nerves and strong will who early showed by her loud impatient cry how she might suffer in after life, if the habit of patience were not timely formed. It was timely formed. She died of scarlet fever before she was four years old; and the self-command that little creature showed amidst the restlessness of her fever and the grievous pain of her sore-throat, was a comfort which will remain for ever to those who mourn her. It of course lessened her own suffering, and it cheered the heart of her wise mother with a joy which lights up her memory. Here the great condition was fulfilled which is essential to the work;—the parents are themselves patient and consistent. Self-control can never be taught without example. From the beginning an infant can perceive whether the moral atmosphere around it is calm or stormy, and will naturally become calm or stormy accordingly. If its mother scolds the servant, if its father gets into a passion with the elder children, if there is disturbance of mind because a meal is delayed,—if voices grow loud and angry in argument, or there is gloom in the face or manner of any grown person who has a headache, how is the infant to learn to wait and be cheerful under its little troubles?—these little troubles being to it misfortunes as great as it is at all able to bear.

I would not cite the old quaker discipline of families as a pattern of what is to be wished in all things. There was too often a want of tenderness, and of freedom and of mirth—such as children, need, and as are quite compatible with the formation of a habit of patience: but in that one respect,—of patience,—how admirable are the examples that many of us have seen! The cultivation of serenity being a primary religious duty with the parents, how the spirit and the habit spread through the children! Before they could understand that the grown people about them were waiting for the guidance of "the Inward Witness," they saw and felt that the temper was that of humble waiting; and they too learned to wait. When set up on a high stool from which they could not get down, and bid to sit still without toys for a prescribed time, how many a restless child learned to subdue his inward chafing, and to sit still till the hand of the clock showed that he might ask to come down! This exercise was a preparation for the silent meeting, where there would be less to amuse his eyes, and no one could tell how long he might have to sit; and how well the majority of quaker children went through this severer test! Few of us will approve of this kind of discipline. We think it bad, because unnatural. We think that the trials of a child's patience which come of themselves every day are quite enough for its powers, and, if rightly used, for its training; but the instance shows how powerful is the example of the parents and the habit of the household in training little children to self-control.

Yes,—the little occasions of every day are quite enough: and if they were not, little could be gained, and much would be lost, by inventing more. There is tyranny in making a lively child sit on a high stool with nothing to do, even though the thing is ordained for its own good; and every child has a keen sense of tyranny. The patience taught by such means cannot be thorough. It cannot be an amiable and cheerful patience, pervading the whole temper. It is much better to use those natural occasions which it is clear that the parent does not create. There is seldom or never a day when something does not happen to irritate a child;—it is hungry, or thirsty, or tired; it gets a tumble, or dislikes cold water, or wants to be petted when its mother is busy; or breaks a toy, or the rain comes when it wants to go out, or pussy runs away from play, or it has an ache or a pain somewhere. All these are great misfortunes for the time to a little child: and if it can learn by degrees to bear them, first by being beguiled of them, and then by being helped through them, and at last by sustaining them alone, there is every hope that the severe trials of after life will be sustained with less effort than is required by these trifles now. A four-year-old child that can turn away and find amusement for itself when its mother cannot attend to it,—and swallow its tears when the rain will not let it sow its garden seeds, and stifle its sobs when it has knocked its elbow, and forgive any one who has broken its toy, and lie still without complaining when it is ill, gives the fairest promise of being able to bear serenely the severest calamities of after life. For my own part, I feel that no spectacle of fortitude in man or woman is more animating and touching than what may be seen in little children, who have seriously entered upon the great work of self-government,—sustained by wise and tender parental help. Some time ago, I was in the house with a little girl of three years old, whose throat was one day very sore. She tried in vain to get down some dinner,—cried, was amused, and went to sleep. On waking, some of the soft rice-pudding from our table was tried; but the throat was now worse, and she cried again. To amuse her, she was set up at our table in her little chair, between her mama and me. I saw the desperate efforts she was making to keep down her sobs: and when she looked over to her father, and said softly "I mean to be dood," it was too much for others besides me. Her tender father helped her well through it. He told her a long long story about something he had seen that morning; and as her large eyes were fixed on his face, the sobs subsided, and she became absorbed in what he was telling her. That child was as truly an object of reverence to us as any patient sufferer of mature age.

The finest opportunity for the cultivation of patience in a household is where there are many children,—boys and girls,—with no great difference of years between them. Here, in the first place, the parents have need of all the faith and patience they have, to bear hopefully with the impatience of some of their children. There are moments, hours, and days, in the best households, when the conscientious and tender mother feels her heart rent by the spectacle of the quarrels of her children. It is a truth which had better be at once fully admitted, that where there are many children nearly approaching each other in age, their wills must clash, their passions become excited, and their affections be for the time over-borne. When a mother sees her children scratch and strike, when her ear catches the bitter words of passion between brothers, her heart stands still with grief and dread. But she must be comforted. All may be well if she overrules this terrible necessity as she may. She must remember that the strength of will thus shown is a great power for use in the acquisition of patience. She must remember that the odiousness of passion is not yet evident to her children, as it is to her. She must remember how small is the moral comprehension of a child, and therefore how intense are its desires, and how strong is the provocation when those desires are thwarted. She must remember that time and enlargement of views are what children want to make them men: and that time and enlargement are sure to come to these young creatures, and make men of them, if the parents do their part. Her part to-day is to separate the children who cannot agree; to give time and opportunity for their passions to subside, the desire of the moment to pass away, and the affections and the reason to be aroused. She must obtain their confidence apart, and bring them together again when they can forgive and agree. If she finds that such troubles enable her to understand her children better, and reveal their own minds to themselves, and if such failures help them to a more careful self-rule, the event may be well worth the pain.

I have said that there are few or no large families of children in which quarrelling does not sometimes occur. But if the quarrelling does not early cease—if the liability does not pass away like the diseases of childhood, it is sadly plain that the fair opportunity of cultivating a habit of patience has been lost or misused. It must be early and watchfully used. Every member of the household must be habituated, constantly and as a privilege, to wait and forbear for the sake of others. The father takes the lead—as he ought to do in all good things. His children see in him, from year to year, an example of patient toil—patient and cheerful toil—whether he be statesman, merchant, farmer, shop-keeper, artizan or labourer. The mother comes next,—seen to wait patiently on her sick or helpless infant, and to be forbearing with servants and children, enduring in illness and fatigue, and cheerful through everything. Then come the elder children, who must have been long and steadily trained, through early self-control, to wait, not only in tenderness on the helpless infant, but in forbearance on the weakness of those younger and frailer than themselves. Then come those of the middle age, who have to wait in such patience as they are capable of under their own personal trials, and the will and pleasure of their parents and elders. And lastly come the little ones, who are likely to have plenty of opportunity for self-command amidst the business and chances of a large family, and the variety of influences ever at work therein. So various a household is a complete little world to children—the discipline of which is no small privilege as being preparatory to that of the larger world upon which they must enter after their habits of mind are formed. To the parents the advantage is inestimable of having this little world, not only under their eye, so that they may timely see how their children are likely to fare morally in the great world of adult life, but under their hand, so that they can, according to their discretion, adapt its influences to the needs of their charge.

Some households,—and not a few—are made a harsh school, or a sweet home of Patience, by the presence of some infirmity of body or mind in some one member. This is a case so frequent, and the circumstance is so important, that I must devote my next pages to it.

# CHAPTER XII.
## CARE OF THE POWERS: PATIENCE—INFIRMITY.

Though the great majority of children born into the world have five senses and four limbs, a full-formed brain, and a well-formed frame, there are many thousands in every civilised country that have not: and so many more thousands are interested in their lot, that it is, or ought to be, a subject of wide and deep concern how their case should be treated, for their own sake, and that of all connected with them. It is a matter of great and increasing surprise, when elections of objects for Blind and Deaf and Dumb Institutions, or a special census for the purpose occurs, how very numerous are the Blind and Deaf and Dumb: and much greater still is the proportion of persons who, through ill health or accident, lose a limb, or grow up deformed. And I believe the cases of total or partial idiotcy are more numerous even than these. The number of persons thus interested in the subject of bodily infirmity is very large indeed; and it would be a great omission in treating of Household Education, not to speak of what concerns so many homes.

The first impulse of a parental heart, on becom ing aware of the infirmity of a child, is to lavish on the sufferer all its tenderness, and thus to strive to compensate to it for what it must forego and suffer from its peculiarity. The impulse, being natural and unselfish, is right; but it is not enough. It is very far indeed from being all that is due to a creature whose helplessness gives it a sacred claim upon its whole race for whatever aid can be afforded it. If it were good that a mother should nurse an infirm child through the day, and guard it all the night:—that she should devote all her time and all her love, and sacrifice all her pleasures to it, and minister to its wishes every hour of its life;—if it were good that she should do all this, it would not be enough. It is not good, and it is not enough.

The true claim of an infirm child, as of every other child, is to be made the most of. And no human being was ever yet made the most of by lavish and unchastened indulgence. Every human being,—not excepting even the idiot,—has a world of its own, wherein to act and enjoy: and the parent's charge is to enable it to act and enjoy in its own world in the fullest and freest manner possible.

Let us take the worst case first:—that of the idiot.

It is never the case that a human being has no faculties at all. A child whose brain did not act at all, could not live. It could not move, nor swallow or digest food, nor see, nor hear, nor breathe. And it seldom or never happens that it has not many faculties, though the want, in an idiot, of what we call Sense makes us too careless in observing what powers he has, and in making what we can of them. From the deficiency of some faculties, and the consequent want of co-operation and balance among his powers, the idiot lacks sense, and must therefore be taken care of all his days, like an infant: but it does not follow that he can never do and enjoy more than an infant. On the contrary, we see, oftener than not, that an idiot has some strong faculties. One may be shockingly gluttonous and sensual: another is desperately orderly: another is always singing: another is wonderful in arithmetic, though nobody can conceive how he learned: another draws every thing he sees: another imitates everything he hears: another is always building clay houses, or cutting wood or paper into shapes: another can always tell the time—day or night—even where there is no clock in the house or within hearing. One will share everything he has to eat with the dog, or the cat, or the bird: another caresses his mother, or brothers and sisters, and follows them about wherever they go; while another gives no heed to anybody, but stands out of doors for hours listening to the wind or the birds, and sits a whole winter evening watching the blazing fire. One will not be ruled, and fights everybody who tries to control him, while another is in a transport or an agony, according as his mother looks pleased or displeased with him. All these tendencies show that some part or other of the brain is alive and active: and it is the parent's business, with this child as with the rest, to make the most that can be made of his brain.

As reason cannot be used in his case, there must be all the more diligence in the use of Habit: and as he has no reason of his own, that of his family must be made available to him to the utmost. He must be made the family charge; and every member of the household must be admitted into the council held in his behalf. There is hardly a child so young but that it can understand the main points of the special training required, and the reasons for them. There is hardly a child so young but that it can understand that John does not know, as other people do, when to leave off eating; and that this is why the proper quantity is set before him, and no more is given: and there are not a few little ones who will refrain from asking for more of a good thing at table because John is to be trained not to ask for more. If the object is to make John clean and tidy, the youngest will bear cold water, and the trouble of dressing cheerfully, that John may see what other people do, and perhaps learn to imitate them. If John ever sings, some little one will begin to sing when John looks dull; and the family will learn as many tunes as they can to give him a variety. If he is fond of arranging things, they will lead him to the cupboard or the play-room, when it wants putting in order. When he mopes, they will bring him the scissors and paper, or the slate and pencil, or they will empty the box of bricks on the floor, that the pleasant rattle may tempt him to come and build. If, happily, the time should arrive when John may learn to do something useful, every one takes pride in it. At worst, he may perhaps be trained to work the mangle, or to turn the wheel at the rope-walk. His faculty of order may be turned to account by letting him set the dinner and tea-table, and clear away. By a faculty of constructiveness, he may become a fair basket-maker. By his power of imitation, he may learn to dig in the field, or to saw wood, or blow glass, or do other such mechanical work. If the whole family not only love their poor brother, but take his interests fairly to heart, his case may be made something of in one way or another. At worst he will probably be saved from being offensive or annoying to those about him;—a thing almost always practicable in cases of idiotcy from birth: and it is very likely that he will be enabled to pass through life, not only harmless, but busy, and, to some extent, useful, and as happy as his deficient nature permits.

This is not a case in which patience can be spoken of as a solace to the individual. He may be saved from the misery of impatience by wise training,—by the formation of habits of quietness, under the rule of steady, gentle authority. This may often be done: but the noble and sweet solace of patience under his restrictions is not for him: for he is unconscious, and does not need it. It remains for those who do need it—for those who suffer for him and by him—for the father who sighs that his son can never enjoy the honour and privilege of toil, or the blessing of a home;—for the mother whose pillow is wet with the tears she sheds over her child's privations;—for the children whose occupations and play are disturbed by the poor brother who wants their playthings, and hides or spoils their books or work. They all have need of much patience; and, under good training, they obtain patience according to their need. From what I have seen, I know that the training of such a being may become a cheerful and hopeful object to his parents, and one which strengthens them to repress his whims and deny his animal appetites, and inflict the pain of their displeasure upon him, in the patient hope of giving him some degree of the privilege of self-government. From what I have seen, I know that the most self-willed and irritable child of such a family may learn never to be angry with John, however passionate at times with others. Toys broken by John are not to be cried for;—work spoiled by John is to be cheerfully done over again: and everybody is to help to train John not to do such mischief again.

Poor John knows nothing of life and its uses. He goes through his share of it, like one walking in a dream, and then passes away without leave-taking. He passes away early; for people in his state rarely live very long. Brain is the great condition of life; and an imperfect brain usually brings early death. It is when he has passed away that the importance of poor John's life becomes felt and understood. Neighbours may and do reasonably call his departure a blessing; and the parents and brethren may and do reasonably feel it an unspeakable relief from anxiety and restraint. But they mourn him with a degree of sorrow surprising to themselves. When the parents mark the habits of self-government, and the temper of cheerful patience, generated in their remaining children, they feel as if under deep obligations to their dead son, as the instrument of this. And the youngest of the tribe looks round wistfully for John, and daily wishes that he was here, to do what he was fond of doing, and enjoy the little pleasures which were looked upon as particularly his own.

If the worst case of infirmity may issue thus, we may turn cheerfully to some which are light in comparison, however sad when looked at by themselves—the cases of blind and deaf children. What is to be made of these?

The case of the deaf is unquestionably the worst of the two, when the deficiency is from birth. The subsequent loss of either sense is quite a different matter. Then, blindness is the severest privation of the two, from its compulsory idleness, and total exclusion from the objects of the lost sense, while the deaf can always be busy in mind and hands, and retain the most important part of the world of sound in written and printed speech. It is the privation of language which makes the case of those born deaf worse than that of the born blind. Those born deaf are dumb; and they are rendered incapable of any high degree of intellectual and moral cultivation, by being cut off from all adequate knowledge of the meaning of language, and from the full reception of most abstract ideas. This is not the place for discussion on this subject. It is enough to say here, that every one who has tried knows that though it is easy to teach a deaf and dumb child what is meant by the words "dog," "sheep," "spoon," "tree," "table," &c., it is found beyond measure difficult to teach it the meaning of "Monday," "Tuesday," "Wednesday," &c., and of "love," "truth," "hatred," "wisdom," and the names of unseen things in general. There is every reason to believe that the most highly educated deaf and dumb persons, who use language readily and prettily, have yet very narrow and superficial minds—from language not being to them natural speech, incessantly bringing them into communication with other minds, but a lesson taught as we teach blind children about colours, which they may speak about without making mistakes, but can never understand.

It is necessary for the parents of the deaf and dumb to be aware of these things, if they are to look their child's lot steadily in the face, and learn what is the best that can be made of it. They must apply themselves chiefly to give it what it is least likely to obtain from others—not so much ideas of sight, touch, smell, and taste, as of unseen things. They must ever bear in mind that the great purpose of the human ear and of speech is not so much to convey ideas of sound—sweet and profitable as is all the natural music of the universe—as of unseen things—of the whole world of the spirit, from which their child is naturally shut out by its infirmity. After all that they can do, there will be a sad deficiency; but they must lessen it as much as they can. There is no fear but that the child will, much as others, enjoy the sights which are laid open to it, and be quick and ready in action, according to its ideas. They must arouse in it the pleasure of using its mental faculties; and more carefully still, the satisfaction of moral energy. They must be even more careful with it than with the rest to lead it on to the exercise of self-denial, and a habit of thoughtful conscientiousness, that it may learn from its own moral expe rience much that it is debarred from learning as others do of the rich kingdom which lies within us all. In this case, above all others, is the moral example of the parents important to the child. Other children hear everyday the spoken testimony of their parents in favour of what is good in morals and manners. They hear it in church, and in every house they enter. The deaf child judges by what it sees, and guides itself accordingly. If it sees bad temper and manners, how is it to know of anything better? If it sees at home only love and kindness, just and gentle, has it not an infinitely better chance of becoming loving and gentle itself?

The parents must keep a careful guard on their own pity for their defective child. A deaf child has scarcely any notion, as a blind one has, of what it loses; and nothing is more certain than that deaf children are apt to be proud and vain, and to take advantage of the pity which everybody feels for them. Knowing little of their own loss, they misunderstand this pity, and are apt to take to themselves the credit of all the notice it brings them, and to grasp at all they can get. A watchful parent knows from her heart that there is no blame in this; but she sees that there is great danger. The child cannot help the liability; but it may be rescued from it. She must not be lavish of indulgence which may be misunderstood. She should let it be as happy as it can in its own way—and the deaf and dumb are usually very brisk and cheerful. What she has to do for it is not to attempt to console it for a privation which it does not feel, but to open to it a higher and better happiness in a humble, occupied, and serene state of mind. She should set before it its own state of privation, notwithstanding any mortification that the disclosure may cause: and when that mortification is painful, she should soothe it by giving, gently and cheerfully, the sweet remedies of humility and patience.

In the case of the blind child, the training must be very different. Every day, and almost every hour, reminds the blind child of its privation; and its discipline is so severe, that almost any degree of indulgence in the parent would be excusable, if it were not clearly the first duty to consider the ultimate welfare of the child. It is natural to the sighing mother to watch over its safety with a nervous anxiety, to go before it to clear its way, to have it always at her knee, and to make everybody and everything give way to it. But she must remember that her child is not destitute, and for ever helpless, because it has one sense less than other people. It has the wide world of the other four senses to live in, and a vaster mental and moral world than it will ever learn fully to use: and she must let it try what it can make of its possessions. She will find that it learns like others that fire burns and that bruises are disagreeable, and that it can save itself from burns and bruises by using its senses of touch and hearing. She will encourage it in the cheerful work of shifting for itself, and doing, as far as possible, what other people do. The wise and benevolent Dr. Howe tells us of the children who come to the Blind School at Boston, that for the first two or three days they are timid and forlorn—having been accustomed to too much care from their mothers, who will not let them cross the floor without being sure that there is nothing in the way. But they presently enter into the free and cheerful spirit of the house, use their faculties, feel their way boldly, and run, climb, swing, and play as merrily as any other children. That school is a little world of people with four senses—not so happy a one as if they had five, but a very good one, nevertheless; sufficiently busy, safe, and cheerful for those who use heartily such powers as they have.

This is the way in which the lot of the blind should be viewed by their parents. And even then the deprivation is quite sad enough to require great efforts of patience on every hand. The parents have need of a deep and settled patience when they see that their child has powers which, if he had but eyes, would make him able and happy in some function from which he is now for ever cut off: and the whole family have need of patience for their infirm member when they are gaining knowledge, or drinking in enjoyment through the eye, while he sits dark, and unconscious or mortified. As for him, in his darkness and mortification, there can be no question of his need of patience. How to aid him and supply this need, I shall consider in my next chapter, when treating of the other infirmities which some children have to learn to bear.

# CHAPTER XIII.
## CARE OF THE POWERS: PATIENCE—INFIRMITY.

The smaller misfortunes which we now turn to, under the head of Infirmity—the loss of a limb, the partial loss of a sense, deformity and sickness—are scarcely less afflictive to the parent than those we have considered, because they are even more trying to the child. The sufferer is fully conscious of these: and the parents' heart is sore at the spectacle of its mortifications. What can be done to help it to a magnanimous patience?

First, there must be the fullest confidence between the parents and the child. It can open its swelling heart to no one else; for the depth of its feeling renders it quite unable to speak of its sufferings to any one, unless allured to do so; and no one can or ought to allure it to this confidence, except its parents, or in case of failure from them. It may be thought strange that this apparently natural act should be set before the parents as a duty: but I speak from knowledge; and from the knowledge of so many cases that I am compelled to believe that the very last subject on which parents and child speak together is that on which it is most necessary to the sufferer to have spoken sympathy. Some parents have not courage to face the case themselves, and evade the painful thought from day to day. Some feel for their child that sort of deference which it is natural to feel for the afflicted, and wait for the sufferer to speak. Some persuade themselves that it is better for the child not to recognise the trial expressly, and repel by forced cheerfulness the sufferer's advances towards confidence. All this is wrong. I have known a little crippled girl grow up to womanhood in daily pain of heart from the keen sense of her peculiarity, almost without uttering a syllable to any human being of that grief which cursed her existence; and suffering in mind and character irreparably from the restraint. She got over it at last, to a considerable degree, and became comparatively free and happy; but nothing could ever compensate to her for her long bondage to false shame, or repair the mischief done to the action of her mind by its being made to bear unrelieved weight which it had naturally power to throw off. I know another sufferer from the same misfortune whose heart was early opened by genial confidence, and who throve accordingly. She had to bear all the pain which a lively and sensitive child must feel in being unable to play and dance as others do, and being so marked an object as to be subject to staring in the street, and to the insulting remarks of rude children as she passed. But the sympathy of her protectors bore her through till her mind was strong enough to protect itself; and she has come out of the struggle free and gay, active and helpful to a marvellous degree—even graceful, making a sort of plaything of her crutch, and giving constant joy to her friends, and relief to strangers, by her total freedom from false shame. I have known deafness grow upon a sensitive child, so gradually as never to bring the moment when her parents felt impelled to seek her confidence; and the moment therefore never arrived. She became gradually borne down in health and spirits by the pressure of her trouble, her springs of pleasure all poisoned, her temper irritated and rendered morose, her intellectual pride puffed up to an insufferable haughtiness, and her conscience brought by perpetual pain of heart into a state of trembling soreness—all this, without one word ever being offered to her by any person whatever of sympathy or sorrow about her misfortune. Now and then, some one made light of it; now and then, some one told her that she mismanaged it, and gave advice which, being inapplicable, grated upon her morbid feelings; but no one inquired what she felt, or appeared to suppose that she did feel. Many were anxious to show kindness, and tried to supply some of her privations; but it was too late. She was shut up, and her manner appeared hard and ungracious while her heart was dissolving in emotions. No one knew when she stole out of the room, exasperated by the earnest talk and merry laugh that she could not share, that she went to bolt herself into her own room, and sob on the bed, or throw herself on her knees, to pray for help or death. No one knew of her passionate longing to be alone while she was, for her good, driven into society; nor how, when by chance alone for an hour or two, she wasted the luxury by watching the lapse of the precious minutes. And when she grew hard, strict, and even fanatical in her religion, no one suspected that this was because religion was her all—her soul's strength under agonies of false shame, her wealth under her privations, her refuge in her loneliness: while her mind was so narrow as to require that what religion was to her—her one pursuit and object—it should be everybody else. In course of years, she, in a great measure, retrieved herself, though still conscious of irreparable mischief done to her nature. All this while, many hearts were aching for her, and the minds of her family were painfully occupied in thinking what could be done for her temper and her happiness. The mistake of reserve was the only thing they are answerable for: a mistake which, however mischievous, was naturally caused by the very pain of their own sympathy first, and the reserve of the sufferer afterwards.

From the moment that a child becomes subject to any infirmity, a special relation between him and his mother begins to exist: and their confi dence must become special. She must watch for, or make occasions for speaking to him about his particular trial; not often, nor much at a time, but so as to leave an opening for the pouring out of his little heart. If he is not yet conscious of his peculiarity, this is the gentlest and easiest way in which he can be made so. If he is conscious, he must have some pain at his heart which he will be the better for confiding. Hump-backed people are generally said to be vain, haughty, fond of dress, forward and talkative, irritable and passionate. If not so, they are usually shy and timid. I cannot see anything in their peculiarity to cause the first-mentioned tendencies: and I believe they arise from the mismanagement of their case. The fond mother and pitying friends may naturally forget that the child does not see himself as they see him, and fancy that they soothe his mortifications by saying whatever they can say in favour of his appearance—letting him know that he has pretty hair, or good eyes. They may even dress him fine, to make up to him in one way for his faults of appearance in another. Under the idea of encouraging him under his supposed mortifications, they may lead him on to be forward and talkative. And then again, his mortifications, when they come upon him unprepared, may well make him irascible. How much of this might be obviated, as well as the shyness and timidity of those who are left to themselves, by timely confidence between the mother and child! When they are alone together, calm and quiet, let her tell him that he does not look like other children, and that he will look less like other people as he grows older. Never let her tell him that this is of no great consequence—never let her utter the cant that is talked to young ladies at schools, that the charms of the mind are everything, and those of the form and face nothing. This is not true; and she ought to know that it is not: and nothing but truth will be strong enough to support him in what he must undergo. Let her not be afraid to tell him the worst. He had better hear it from her; and it will not be too much for him, if told in a spirit of cheerful patience. The child, like the man, never has a happier hour than that which succeeds the reception of bad news, if the nobler faculties are allowed their free play. If such a child hears from his mother that he will always be ugly-shaped and odd-looking,—that he will not be able to play as other boys do, or will be laughed at when he tries; that he will be mocked at and called "My lord" in the streets, and so on, and yet that all these things will not make him unhappy if he can bear them; and if they go on to consult how he may bear them, and she opens out to him something of the sweet pleasures of endurance, he will come out of the consultation exhilarated, and perhaps proudly longing to meet his mortifications, and try his strength. Such pride must have a fall,—like all the pride of childhood,—and many an hour of depression must he know for every one of exhilaration: but his case is put into his own hands, and there is every hope that he will conquer, through patience, at last. And what a refuge he has in his mother! How well she will now know his feelings and his needs! and how easy and natural it will be to him henceforth to confide in her! And her knowledge of his secret mind will enable her to oversee and regulate the conduct of the rest of the household towards him, so as to guard against his being treated with an indulgence which he can dispense with, or his receiving in silence wounds to his feelings which might rankle. The object is, with sufferers under every kind of conscious infirmity, to make them hardy in mind,—saving them from being hardened. They must know in good time that they have a difficult and humbling lot, and what its difficulties and humiliations are,—their noblest faculties being at the same time roused to meet them. It is the rousing of these noble faculties which makes the hour of confidence one of exhilaration: and when the actual occasion of trial arises, when the cripple is left out of the cricket-match, and the deaf child misses the joke or entertaining story, and the hump-back hears the jibe behind him,—there is hope that the nobler faculties will be obedient to the promised call, and spread the calm of patience over the tumult of the sufferer's soul.

But, while the infirm child is encouraged to take up the endurance of his infirmity as an object and an enterprise, he must not be allowed to dwell too much on it, nor on the peculiar features of his condition; or his heroism will pass over into pride, and his patience into self-complacency. Life and the world are before him, as before others; and one circumstance of lot and duty, however important, must not occupy the place of more than one,—either in his confidences with his mother, or in his own mind. The more he is separated from others by his infirmity, the more carefully must his interests and duties be mixed up with those of others, in the household and out of it. Companionship in every way must be promoted all the more, and not the less, because of the eternal echo within him, "The heart knoweth its own bitterness, and the stranger intermeddleth not with its joy."

What has been said thus far about patience will serve for cases of sickness, as well as for other trials among children. I may add that I think it a pity to lavish indulgence—privileges—upon a sick child, for two reasons;—that such indulgence is no real comfort or compensation to the suffering child, who is too ill to enjoy it: and that it is witnessed by others, and remembered by the patient himself when he has forgotten his pain, so as to cause sickness to be regarded as a state of privilege; a persuasion likely to lead to fancies about health, and an exaggeration of ailments. All possible tenderness, of course, there should be, and watchfulness to amuse the mind into forgetfulness of the body: but the less fuss and unusual indulgence the better for the child's health of body and mind, and the purer the lesson of patience which he may bring out of his sickness. Illness is a great evil, little to be mitigated by any means of diversion that can be used: and a child usually trained to patience, may be trusted to bear the evil well, if not misled by false promises: and it is much kinder to him to let him rest on a quiet and steady tenderness, than to promise and offer him indulgences which will be longed for hereafter, but which wholly disappoint him now, and add another trial to the many which put his patience to the proof.

# CHAPTER XIV.

## CARE OF THE POWERS.—LOVE.

It appears to me, that much disappointment in the results of education, as in other departments of life, arises from the confusion we fall into about human affections,—mixing up things which do not belong to each other, and then being disappointed at a mixed result. For instance, we speak of love as if it were one affection; or at most of two kinds—one a passion and the other an affection: whereas, there are many kinds of love, as distinct from one another as hope and patience. Besides what is commonly called the passion of love, there are other kinds which differ as essentially from one another, as from this. It is commonly, but as I think, hastily, supposed that a child's love of her doll is the same affection which will be fixed hereafter on a schoolfellow, on her parents, and on suffering fellow-creatures. It is supposed to be the same affection, employed on different objects: and the parent is perplexed and shocked when the little creature who cannot be parted from her doll, shows indifference towards her family, and has no sympathy with a beggar, or a sick neighbour. If the parents will put away their perplexity and dismay, and set themselves to learn from what is before their eyes, they may discover what will comfort and direct them.

With the passion of love, as it is called, we have nothing to do here, but to give an anecdote by the way. A little girl was telling a story to her father, when they fell in with the kind of perplexity, I have spoken of. She told of a knight who once loved a lady, and of all the hard and troublesome things the knight did to gratify the wishes of the lady: and how, at last, when the lady did not choose to marry him, he carried her off, and shut her up in a castle, and gave her everything he could think of to make her happy: but she could not enjoy all these fine things, because she pined to get home. "Oh!" said the father, "she did wish to get out, then." "Yes! she begged and prayed of the knight to let her go home: but he loved her so much that he would not." "Well: but you said he did everything he could to gratify her: why was that?" "Because he loved her so much." "What! he did everything to please her because he loved her so much: and then he would not let her go home as she wished, because he loved her so much! How can that be?" The child thought for awhile, and then said "I suppose he had two loves for her: and one made him do almost everything that she liked; and the other made him want that she should do what he liked."

If parents could see thus plainly the difference between the several kinds of love which their children should experience, it would be well for all parties. A mother who intensely loves her little prattler, is mortified that the child appears to have but a very moderate love for her in return: and she comforts herself with the hope that the child's affection will strengthen as it grows, till it becomes a fair return for her own. She does not perceive that the child already entertains an affection much like her own,—only, not for her, but for something else. A little girl who had to lose her leg, promised to try to lie still if she might have her doll in her arms: and wonderfully still she lay, clasping her doll. When it was over, the surgeon thoughtlessly said, "Now shall I cut off your doll's leg?" "Oh! no, no!" cried the child, in an agony of mind far greater than she had shown before: "not my doll's leg;—don't hurt my doll!" And she could hardly be comforted. Here was an affection the same as the mother's,—and as strong and true: but of a different kind from that which children can ever feel for parents; for it is purely instinctive, while the love of children for parents is made up of many elements, and must slowly grow out of not only a natural power of attachment, but a long experience of hope, reliance, veneration and gratitude.

This instinctive love is a pretty thing to witness: as in the case of a very little child who had a passionate love of flowers. She would silently carry out her little chair in the summer morning, and sit down in the middle of the flower-bed, and be overheard softly saying, "Come you little flower—open, you little flower! When will you open your pretty blue eye?" This is charming; and so it is to see an infant fondling a kitten, or feeding the brood of chickens, and a girl singing lullaby to her doll. But it must ever be remembered, that this is the lowest form of human affection till it is trained into close connection with the higher sentiments. What it is when left to itself—and it will too probably be left to itself by parents who are satisfied with any manifestation of affection in children;—what it is when left to itself may be seen in some disgusting spectacles which occasionally meet our eyes among the mature and the old. We see it in the young mother who spoils her child—who loves her child with so low a love, that she indulges it to its hurt. We see it in the aged mother, who loves her manly son as a bear loves its cub;—only with more selfishness, for she cannot consider his good, but lavishes ill-humour and fondness on him by turns. We see it in the man who gives his mind to the comfort of his horse; and never a look or a word to a hungry neighbour. We see it in a woman, who opens her arms to every dog or cat that comes near her, whose eye brightens, and whose cheek mantles while she feeds her canaries, though she never had a friendship, nor cares for any human being but such as are under five years old.

Thus low is this instinctive affection when left to itself. But it is inestimable when linked on to other and higher kinds of love, and especially to that which is the highest of all, and worthy to gather into itself all the rest,—benevolence. It is easy to form this link when its formation is desired: and it is terribly easy to neglect it when its importance is not perceived. The child must be led to desire the good of the cat, or bird, or doll, to the sacrifice of its own inclinations. It must not hurt pussy, or throw dolly into a corner, (every child believing that dolly can feel) nor frighten the bird: and moreover, it must be made to discharge punctually, even to its own inconvenience, the duty of feeding the live favourite, and cherishing the doll. This leads on naturally to a cherishing and forbearing love of the baby-brother or sister: and next, perhaps, the parents may be surprised by an offer of affection in sickness which never showed itself while they were in health. A child who receives caresses carelessly, or runs away from them to caress the kitten, (which, perhaps, runs away in its turn,) will come on tiptoe to his mother's knee when she is ill, and stroke her face, or nurse her foot in his lap, or creep up into her easy chair, and nestle there quietly for an hour at a time: and yet perhaps this same child will appear as indifferent as before when his mother is well again, and does not seem to want his good offices.

From home, the affection may next be led a little further abroad. This must be done very cautiously, and the expansion of benevolence by no means hurried or made a task of. I knew a little girl who, at four years old, was full of domestic benevolence—capable of denying herself noise and amusement on fitting occasions, and never happier than when waiting on and cherishing a sick person. One day she seemed so much interested about a poor woman who had come to beg, that her mother took her into consultation about what could be done for the woman and her children. When told how nearly naked the poor children were, and how they had no more clothes to put on, though the weather was growing colder and colder, she was asked whether she would not like to give her blue frock to one of them. In a low earnest voice, she said "No." The case was again represented to her; and when, with some little shrinking, she again said "No," her mother saw that she had gone rather too far, and had tried the young faculty of benevolence beyond its strength. She watched and waited, and is repaid. In her daughter, warm domestic affections co-exist with a more than ordinary benevolence.

This benevolence is the third form in which we have already seen what is called love. Can any thing be more clearly marked than the difference between these three;—the love that leads to marriage; fondness for objects which can be idolised; and benevolence which has no fondness in it, but desires the diffusion of happiness, and acts independently of personal regards? None of these yield the sort of affection which the heart of the parent desires, and which is essential to family happiness. A child may kill its pet bird, or cat, with kindness, and go out into the street in the early morning, with its halfpenny in its hand (as I have known a child do) to do good with it to somebody;—a child may have these two kinds of love strong in him, and yet show but a weak attachment to the people about him. This attachment is another kind of love from those we have been considering. It is all-important to the character of the individual, and to the happiness of the family circle: and it is therefore of consequence that its nature should be understood, and its exercise wisely cared for.

It is some time before the infant shows attachment to any one. There are many signs of hope and fear in an infant before it gives any token of affection; its arms are held out first to its nurse; and she usually continues the one to whom the child clings, and from whom it will not be separated. Beyond the nurse, the child's attachments sometimes appear unaccountable. It will be happy with some one person in the house, and make a difficulty of going to any one else: and the reason of this may not be plain to anybody. Happy is the mother if she be the one; and a severe trial it is to a loving mother when she is not the one. Of course, if the misfortune be owing to any fault in herself,—if she be irritable, stern, or in any way teasing to the child,—she cannot wonder that he does not love her. If she be tender, gentle, playful, and wise, and still her child loves some one else in the house better, it is a sore trial, certainly; but it must be made the best of. Of course, the mother will strive to discover what it is in another person that attaches the child; and if she can attain the quality, she will. But it is probably that which cannot be attained by express efforts,—a power of entering into the little mind, and meeting its thoughts and feelings. Some persons have this power naturally much more than others; and practice may have given them great facility in using it; while the sense of inexperience, and the strong anxiety that a young mother has, may easily be a restraint on her faculties in dealing with her child. I have heard the mothers of large families declare (in the most private conversation) in so many instances, that their younger children are of a higher quality than the older, and this from an age so early as to prevent the difference being attributed to experience in teaching, that I have been led to watch and think on the subject: and I think that one powerful cause is that the mother has naturally more freedom and playfulness and tact in her intercourse with her younger children than with the elder, and thereby fixes their attachment more strongly: and there are no bounds to the good which arises from strong affections in a child. Happy the mother who is the object of her child's strongest love from the beginning!—happy, that is, if she makes a good use of her privilege. She must never desire more love than the child has to give. The most that it can give will be less than she would like, and far less than her own for it: but she will not obtain more, but only endanger what she has, by making the child conscious of his affections, and by requiring tokens which do not manifest themselves spontaneously. It should be enough for a mother that her child comes to her with his little troubles and pleasures, and shows by his whole behaviour that she is of more importance to him than any one else in the world. If it be so, there will be times when he will spring into her lap, and throw his arms round her neck, and give her the thrilling kiss that she longs to have every day and every hour. But the sweetness of these caresses will be lost when they cease to be spontaneous; and the child will leave off springing into the lap, if it is to be teased for kisses when there. There are few products of the human mind which are to be had good upon compulsion; and affection least of all. I knew a little boy who was brought home from being at nurse in the country, and shown to his conscientious, anxious, but most formal mother. The child clung to his nurse's neck, hid his face on her shoulder, and screamed violently. But his mother's voice was heard above his noise, saying solemnly, "Look at me, my dear. Nurse is going away, and you will not see her any more. You must love me now." Whether she thus gained her child's love, my readers may conjecture.

The mother who is first in her child's affection is under the serious responsibility of imparting the treasure to others. She takes her whole household into her own heart; and she must open her little one's heart to take in all likewise. She must associate all in turn in his pursuits and pleasures, till his love has spread through the house, and he can be happy and cherished in every corner of it.

The mother who sees some one else more beloved than herself,—the servant, perhaps, or an elder child of her own,—must not lose heart, much less temper, or all is lost. It is possible that her turn may never come: but it is far more probable that it will, if she knows how to wait for it. She must go on doing her part as perseveringly and, if it may be, as cheerfully as if her heart was satisfied; and sooner or later the child will discover, never to forget, what a friend she is. Moreover, if her mind and manner are not such as to win a child in his early infancy, they may suit his needs at a later stage of his mind. I have observed that the mothers who are most admirable at some seasons of their children's lives fall off at others. I have seen a mother who had extraordinary skill in bringing out and training her children's faculties before they reached their teens, and who was all-sufficient for them then, fail them sadly as a friend and companion in the important years which follow seventeen. And I have seen a mother who could make no way with her children in their early years, and who keenly felt how nearly indifferent they were to her, while her whole soul and mind were devoted to them,—I have seen such a mother idolised by her daughters when they became wise and worthy enough to have her for a friend. I mention these things for comfort and encouragement: and who is more in need of comfort and encouragement than the mother who, loving her child as mothers should, meets with not only a less than adequate, but a less than natural return?

There is one case more sad and more solemn than this; the case of the unloving and unloved child. There are some few human beings in whom the power of attachment is so weak that they stand isolated in the world, and seem doomed to a hermit existence amidst the very throng of human life. If such are neglected, they are lost. They must sink into a slough of selfishness, and perish. And none are so likely to be neglected as those who neither love nor win love. If such an one is not neglected, he may become an able and useful being, after all; and it is for the parents to try this, in a spirit of reverence for his mysterious nature, and of pity for the privations of his heart. They will search out and cherish, by patient love, such little power of attachment as he has: and they will perhaps find him capable of general kindliness, and the wide interests of benevolence, though the happiness of warm friendships and family endearment is denied him. Such an one can never take his place among the highest rank of human beings, nor can know the sweetest happiness that life can yield. But by the generous love of his parents, and of all whom they can influence to do his nature justice, his life may be made of great value to himself and others, and he may become respected for his qualities, as well as for his misfortune.

# CHAPTER XV.
## CARE OF THE POWERS.—VENERATION.

Among the great blessings which are shared by the whole human race, one of the chief is its universal power of veneration.

I call this a universal power, because there is no human being, (except the idiot) in whom it is not inherent from his birth: and I think I may say, that there is none in whom it does not exist, more or less, till his death. Unhappy influences may check or pervert it: but there is no reason to believe that it can be utterly destroyed. The grinning scoffer, who laughs at everything serious, who despises every man but himself, and who is insensible to the wonders and charms of nature, yet stands in awe of something,—if it be nothing better than rank and show, or brute force, or the very power of contempt in others which he values so much in himself. Send for such an one into the presence of the Queen, or bring him to the bar of the House of Commons, or ask him to dinner in a sumptuous palace, and, however far gone he may be in contempt, he will be awe-struck. Set him down face to face with a man who makes game of everything he does not understand, (and that will be almost everything that exists) and he will have a respect for that man. If you can bring his mind into contact with any objects low enough to excite his degraded faculty of veneration, you will find that the faculty is still there. It appears to be indeed inextinguishable.

We have, as usual, two things to take heed to in regard to this great and indispensable power of the mind. First, to take care that the power neither runs riot, nor is neglected. And next, to direct it to its proper objects.

I. The faculty, like all others, is of unequal strength in different people;—in children, as well as in grown persons. We see one man who seems to have no self-reliance or freedom of action in anything; whose life is one long ague fit of superstition, from that cowardly dread of God which he means for religion: who takes anybody's word for everything, from a fear of using his own faculties, and who is overwhelmed in the presence of rank, wealth, or ability superior to his own. We see another man careless, and contemptuous, and self-willed, from a want of feeling of what there is in the universe, and in his fellow-men superior to his faculties, and mysterious to his understanding. And in the merest infants, we may discern, by careful watching, a difference no less marked. One little creature will reach boldly after everything it sees, and buffet its playthings and the people about it, and make itself heard and attended to whenever it so pleases, and has to be taught and trained to lie quiet and submissive. And another of the same age will watch with a shrinking wonder whatever is new or mysterious, and be shy before strangers, and has to be taught and trained to examine things for itself, and to make free with the people about it. Such being the varieties in the strength of the natural faculty, the training of it must vary accordingly.

As I have said before, no human faculty needs to be repressed; because no human faculty is in itself bad. Where any one power appears to be excessive, we are not to set to work to vex and mortify it: but rather, to bring up to it those antagonist faculties which ought to balance it, and which, in such a case, clearly want strengthening. If, for instance, a child appears to have too much of this faculty of Veneration—if it fancies a mystery in everything that happens, and yields too easily to its companions, and loves ghost stories which yet make it ill, and is always awe-struck and dreaming about something or other—that child is not to be laughed at, nor to be led to despise or make light of what it cannot understand. That child has not too much Veneration: for no one can ever have too much of the faculty. The mischief lies in his having too little of something else;—too little self-respect; too little hope; too little courage.

Let him continue to exercise and enjoy freely his faculty of Wonder. His mother should tell him of things that are really wonderful and past finding out: and as he grows old enough, let her point out to him that all things in nature are wonderful, and past our finding out, from the punctuality of the great sun and blessed moon, to the springing of the blade of grass. Let her sympathise in his feeling that there is something awful in the thunderstorm, and in the incessant roll of the sea. Let her express for him, as far as may be, his unutterable sense of the weakness and ignorance of child or man in the presence of the mighty, ever-moving universe, and of the awful unknown Power which is above and around us, wherever we turn. Let her show respect to every sort of superiority, according to its kind—to old age, to scholarship, to skill of every sort, to social rank and office; and above all, to the superiority that goodness gives. Let her thus cherish and indulge her child's natural faculty, and permit no one else to thwart it. But she must give her utmost pains to exercise at the same time his inquiring and knowing faculties, and his courage and self-respect. Among the many wonders which she cannot explain, there are many which she can. He should be encouraged to understand as much as anybody understands, and especially of those things which he is most likely to be afraid of. He should be made to feel what power is given to him by such knowledge: and led to respect this power in himself as he would in any one else. I knew a little child whose reverence for Nature was so strong as almost to overpower some other faculties. She was town-bred: and whenever it chanced that she was out in the country for more than a common walk, she was injuriously excited, all day long. She was not only in a state of devout adoration to the Maker of all she saw: but she felt towards the trees, and brooks, and corn-fields as if they were alive, and she did not dare to interfere with them. One day, some companions carried home some wild strawberry roots for their gardens, and persuaded her to do the same. She did so, in a great tremor. Before she had planted her roots, she had grown fond of them, as being dependent on her; and she put them into the ground very tenderly and affectionately. As it was now near noon, of course she found her strawberries withered enough when she next went to look at them, as they lay drooping in the hot sun. She bethought herself, in her consternation, of a plan for them: ran in for a little chair: put it over the roots, stuffing up with grass every space which could let the sunshine in; watered the roots, and left them, with the sense of having done a very daring thing. It was sunset before she could go to her garden again. When she removed the chair, there were the strawberries, fresh and strong, with leaves of the brightest green! It was a rapturous moment to this superstitious child—this, in which she felt that she had meddled with the natural growth of something, and with success. And it was a profitable lesson. She took to gardening, and to trying her power over Nature in other ways, losing some superstition at every step into the world of knowledge, and gaining self-respect (a highly necessary direction of the spirit of reverence) with every proof of the power which knowledge confers.

What the parent has to do for the child in whom the sentiment of Reverence appears disproportionate, is to give him Power in himself, in every possible way, that he may cease to be overwhelmed with the sense of power out of himself on every hand. If he can become possessed of power of Conscience, his religious fear will become moderated to wholesome awe. If he can become possessed of power of understanding, the mysteries of Nature will stimulate instead of depressing his mind. If he can attain to power of sympathy, he will see men as they are, and have a fellow-feeling with them, through all the circumstances of rank and wealth which once wore a false glory in his eyes. If he can attain a due power of self-reliance, he will learn that his own wonderful faculties and unbounded moral capacities should come in for some share of his reverence, and be brought bravely into action in the universe, instead of being left idle by the wayside, making obeisance incessantly to everything that passes by, while they ought to be up and doing.

What should be done with the pushing, fearless child, who seems to stand in awe of nobody, is plain enough. As I have said, he reverences something: for no human being is without the faculty. His parents must find out what it is that does excite his awe: and, however strange may be the object, they must sympathise in the feeling. I have known a fearless child of three reverence his brother of four and a half. We may laugh; but it was no laughing matter, but a very interesting one, to see the little fellow watch every movement of his brother, give him credit for profound reasons in everything he did, and humbly imitate as much as he could. Supposing such a child to be deficient generally in reverence, it would be a tremendous mistake in the parents to check this one exercise of it. They should, in such a case, carefully observe the rights of seniority among the children; avoid laughing at the follies of the elder, or needlessly pointing out his faults, in the presence of the younger, while they daily strive to raise the standard of both. They must also lead the imagination of the little one to contemplate things which he must feel to be at once real and beyond his comprehension. They must, at serious moments, lead his mind higher than he was aware it would go, even till it sinks under his sense of ignorance. They must carry his thoughts down into depths which he never dreamed of, and where the spirit of awe will surely lay hold upon him. I do not believe there is any child who cannot be impressed with a serious, plain account of some of the wonders of nature; with a report, ever so meagre, of the immensity of the heavens, whose countless stars, the least of which we cannot understand, are for ever moving, in silent mystery, before our eyes. I do not believe there are many children that may not be deeply impressed by the great mystery of brute life, if their attention be duly fixed upon it. Let the careless and confident child be familiarised, not only with the ant and the bee for their wonderful instinct, but with all living creatures as inhabitants of the same world as himself, and at the same time, of a world of their own, as we have; a world of ideas, and emotions, and pleasures, which we know nothing whatever about,—any more than they know the world of our minds. I do not believe there is any child who would not look up with awe to a man or woman who had done a noble act,—saved another from fire or drowning, or told the truth to his own loss or peril, or visited the sick in plague-time, or the guilty in jail. I do not believe there is any child who would not look up with awe to a man who was known to be wise beyond others; to have seen far countries; to have read books in many languages; or to have made discoveries among the stars, or about how earth, air, and water are made. If it be so, who is there that may not be impressed at last by the evident truth that all that men have yet known and done is as nothing compared with what remains to be known and done: that the world-wide traveller is but the half-fledged bird flitting round the nest: that the philosopher is but as the ant which spends its little life in bringing home half a dozen grains of wheat: and that the most benevolent man is grieved that he can do so little for the solace of human misery, feeling himself like the child who tries to wipe away his brother's tears, but cannot heal his grief! Who is there that cannot be impressed by the grave pointing out of the mystery of life, and the vastness of knowledge which lie around and before him; and by the example of him who did none but noble and generous deeds, and bore the fiercest sufferings, and felt contempt for nothing under heaven! How can it but excite reverence to show that he, even he, was himself full of reverence, and incapable of contempt!

II. Having said thus much about nourishing and balancing the faculty of reverence, I need only point out the directions in which it should be trained.

The point on which a child's veneration will first naturally fix will be Power. It must be the parents' first business to fix that veneration on Authority, instead of mere power. Instead of the power to shut up in a closet, or to whip, the child must reverence the authority which reveals itself in calm control and gentle command. The parents must be the first objects of the child's disciplined reverence. Even here, in this first clear case, the faculty cannot work well without sympathy: and the child must have sympathy from the parents themselves. He must see that his parents respect each other; that they consider one another's authority unquestionable in the household; and that they reverence their parent—if Granny be still among them.

Beyond this, there is no reason why the sympathy between parents and children should not be simple, constant, and true, as to their objects of reverence.

The child may revere as very wise, some person whom the parents know not to be so: but they may join their child in revering the wisdom which they know to be his ideal. The child may go into an enthusiasm about some questionable hero,—the exemplar of some virtue which the parents feel to be of a rather low order: but they will sympathise in the homage to virtue—which is the main point. They may be secretly amused at their child's reverence for the constable: but they feel the same in regard to that of which the constable is the representative to the child—the Law. They will lead him on with them in their advancing reverence for knowledge; for that moral and intellectual knowledge united which constitute wisdom; and will thus turn away his regards from dwelling too much on outward distinctions, which might otherwise inspire undue awe.

Yet nearer will their hearts draw to his in veneration for goodness; for intrepid truthfulness, for humble fidelity, for cheerful humility, for gentle charity. And at the ultimate point, their hearts must become one with his; in the presence of the Unknown; for there we are all,—the oldest and the youngest—the wisest and the weakest,—but little children, waiting to learn, and desiring to obey.

# CHAPTER XVI.

## CARE OF THE POWERS.—TRUTHFULNESS.

We come now to consider a moral quality whose importance cannot be overrated, yet about which there is more unsettledness of view and perplexity of heart among parents than about, perhaps, any other. Every parent is anxious about the truthfulness of his child: but whether this virtue is to come by nature, or by gift, or by training, many an one is sorely perplexed to know. So few children are truthful in all respects and without variation, that we may well doubt whether the quality can be inborn. And the cases are so many of children otherwise good—even conscientious in other respects—who talk at random, and say things utterly untrue, that I do not wonder that those who hold low views of human nature consider this a constitutional vice, and a hereditary curse. I am very far from believing this: and I will plainly say what I do believe.

I believe that the requisites of a habit of truthfulness lie in the brain of every child that is born; but that the truthfulness itself has to be taught, as the speech which is to convey it has to be taught; by helping the child to the use of his natural powers. The child has by nature the ear, the lungs, the tongue, the palate, and the various and busy mind,—the requisites for speech: but he does not speak unless incited by hearing it from others, and by being himself led on to attain the power. In a somewhat resembling manner, every child has more or less natural sense of what is just in feeling and action, and what is real in nature, and how to present his ideas to another mind. Here are the requisites to truthfulness of speech: but there is much to be learned, and much to overcome, before the practice of truthfulness can be completely formed, and firmly established. If the case is once understood, we shall know how to set about our work, and may await the event without dismay in the worst cases, though in all with the most careful vigilance.

Is it not true that different nations, even Christian nations, vary more in regard to truthfulness than perhaps any other moral quality? Is it not true that one or two continental nations fall below us in regard to this quality, while they far excel us in kindliness and cheerfulness of temper, and pleasantness of manners? And does not this difference arise from their thinking kindliness and cheerfulness more important than sincerity and accuracy of speech? And is not our national superiority in regard to the practice of truth chiefly owing to its being our national point of honour, and our fixed supposition as a social habit? Do not these facts tend to show that the practice of truthfulness is the result of training? and that we may look for it with confidence as the result of good training?

Now, what are the requisites, and what the difficulties that we have to deal with?

Has not every child a keen sense of right and justice, which he shows from the earliest time that he can manifest any moral judgment at all? He may be injurious and unjust to another, from selfishness and passion: but can he not feel injustice done to himself with the infallibility of an instinct, and claim his rights with the acuteness of a lawyer? Is there anything more surprising to us in the work of education than every child's sense of his rights, and need of unerring justice, till he is far enough advanced generously to dispense with it? Here we have the perception of moral truth for one requisite.

Another requisite is such good perceptive power as informs a child truly of outward facts. There is no natural power which varies more in different subjects than this. One child sees everything as it is, within its range. Another child sees but little, being taken up with what it thinks or imagines. A third sees wrongly, being easily deceived about colours and forms, and the order in which things happen, from its senses being dull, or its faculties of observation being indolent. I have known a child declare an object to be green when it was grey; or a man in a field to be a giant; or a thing to have happened in the morning which took place in the afternoon: and one need but observe how witnesses in a court of justice vary in their testimony about small matters regarding which they are quite disinterested, to see that the same imperfection in the perceptive faculties goes on into mature age. It is plain that these faculties must be exercised and trained very carefully, if the child is to be made accurate in its statements.

Another and most important requisite is that the child should, from the beginning, believe that truthfulness is a duty. This belief must be given on authority: for the obligation to truth is not, as I have said, instinctive, but a matter of reasoning, such as a child is not capable of entering into. He will receive it, easily and permanently, from the assurance and example of his parents; but he does not, in his earliest years, see it for himself. An affectionate child, thinking of a beloved person, will tell his parent that he has just seen and talked with that person, who is known to be a hundred miles off. The parent is shocked: and truly there is cause for distress; for it is plain that the child has as yet no notion of the duty of truthfulness; but the parent must not, in his fear, aggravate the case, and run into the conclusion that the child loves lying. The case probably is that he says what is pleasant to his affections, without being aware that there is a more serious matter to be attended to first: a thing which he may hereafter be shocked not to have known. I happen to remember at this moment, three persons, now conscientiously truthful, who in early childhood were in the habit of telling, not only wonderful dreams, but most wonderful things that they had seen in their walks, on the high-road or the heath; giants, castles, beautiful ladies riding in forests, and so on. In all these cases, the parents were deeply distressed, and applied themselves accordingly, first to check the practice of narration, and next to exercise the perceptive and reflective powers of the children, so as to enable them to distinguish clearly the facts they saw from the visions they called up before their mind's eye. The appeal to conscience they left for cases where their child had clearer notions of right and wrong. Any one of these children would, I believe, at that very time, have suffered much rather than say what he knew to be false, from any motive of personal fear or hope. As I said, all these three are now eminently honourable and trustworthy persons.

The chief final requisite is, of course, conscientiousness. When the child becomes capable of self-knowledge and self-government, this alone can be relied on for such a confirmation of the habit of truth telling, or such a correction of any tendency to inaccuracy, as may carry the young probationer through all temptations from within and from without, steady in the practice of strict truth. When all these requisites are combined,—when the child feels truly, sees truly, and is aware of the duty of speaking truly, the practice of truthfulness becomes as natural and unfailing as if it originated in an instinct.

I remember an instance of the strange, unbalanced, unprincipled state of mind of a child, who was capable of telling a lie, and persisting in it, at the very time that she was conscientious to excess about some of her duties, and her sense of justice (in regard to her own rights) ran riot in her. It is an odd and a sad story; but instructive from its very strangeness. She was asked by her mother one day whether she had not played battledore and shuttlecock before breakfast. From some levity or inattention at the moment, she said "No," and was immediately about to correct herself when her mother's severe countenance roused her pride and obstinacy, and she wickedly repeated her denial. Here it was temper that was the snare. There was nothing to be afraid of in saying the truth, no reason why she should not. But she had a temper of such pride and obstinacy that she was aware of even enjoying being punished, as giving her an opportunity of standing out; while the least word of appeal to her affections or her conscience, if uttered before her temper was roused, would melt her in a moment. The question was repeated in many forms; and still she, with a terrified and miserable conscience, persisted that she had not played battledore that morning; whereas her mother had heard it, and knew from her companion who it was that had played. The lying child was sent to her own room, where she was in consternation enough till a mistake of management was made which spoiled everything, and destroyed the lesson to her. She was sent for to read aloud, before the family, the story of Ananias and Sapphira. She was sobbing so that the reading was scarcely possible, till her thoughts took a turn which speedily dried her tears, and filled her with an insolent indignation which excluded all chance of repentance. She well knew the story of Ananias and Sapphira; and she happened to have a great admiration of the plan of the early Christians, of throwing all their goods into a common stock. She knew that the sin of Ananias and his wife lay chiefly in the selfish fraud which was the occasion of their lie, and that their case was therefore no parallel for hers: and in the indignation of having it supposed that she had sinned in their way,—she who longed above everything to have been an early Christian (a pretty subject truly!)—that she could be thought silly enough to suppose that they were struck dead for their fib, and not for their fraud,—in this insolent indignation she put her one sin out of sight, and felt herself an injured person. This adventure certainly did not strengthen her regard to truth. She dared not state her objection to the story in her own case: and perhaps she also disdained to do it: she remained sullen; and her mother had at last to let the matter drop.

This was a case to make any parent's heart sink: but the worse the case, the more instructive to us now. Here was sufficient moral sense and insight, in one direction, to hear an appeal, if any had been made. Disgrace was the worst possible resort, and especially when untenable ground was taken for it. The best resort would have been a tender and solemn private conversation, in which the entanglement of passionate feelings might have been unravelled, and the seat of moral disease have been explored. When a moral disease so fearful as this appears, parents should never rest till they have found the seat of it, and convinced the perilled child of the deadly nature of its malady. In this case, the child was certainly not half-convinced, and morally worse after the treatment, while the material for conviction, repentance and reformation, was in her.

The method of training must depend much on the organisation of the child in one respect; whether he is ingenuous and frank, or reserved and (I must say it)—sly. Some children are certainly prone to slyness by nature; but there is no reason why, under a wise training, they should not be as honourable as the most ingenuous soul that ever was born. And they may even, when thoroughly principled, be more reliable than some open-minded persons, from being more circumspect.

There is something very discouraging in seeing little creatures who ought to be all fearlessness and confidence hiding things under their pinafores, or slipping out at the back-door for a walk which they might have honestly by asking for it; or putting round-about questions when plain ones would do; or keeping all their little concerns to themselves while spending their whole lives among brothers and sisters. If one looks forward to their maturity, one recoils from the image of what they will be. But they must not grow up with these tendencies. Their fault may turn to virtue, under wise and gentle treatment. Their confidence must be tenderly won, and their innocent desires gratified, while every slyness is quietly shown to be as unavailing as it is disagreeable, and every movement towards ingenuousness cheerfully and lovingly encouraged. The child's imagination must be engaged on behalf of everything that is noble, heroic, and openly glorious before the eyes of men. His conscience and affections must be appealed to, not in words, but by a long course of love and trust, to return the trust he receives. Of course, the parental example must be that of perfect openness and simplicity; for the sight of mystery and concealment in the house is enough to make even the ingenuous child sly, through its faculty of imita tion, and its ambition to be old and wise; and much more will it hinder the expansion of a reserved and cunning child. If these things be all attended to—if he sees only what is open, free, and simple, and receives treatment which is open, free, and encouraging, while it convinces him of a sagacity greater than his own, there is every hope that he will yield himself to the kindly influences dispensed to him, and find for himself the comfort and security of ingenuousness, and turn his secretive ingenuity to purposes of intellectual exercise, where it may do much good and no harm. That ingenuity and sagacity may be well employed among the secrets of history, the complexities of the law, or the mysteries of mechanical construction or chemical analysis, which may make a man vicious and untrustworthy, if allowed to work in his moral nature, and to shroud his daily conduct.

As for the training of the candid and ingenuous child, it is of course far easier and pleasanter; but it must not be supposed that no care is required to make him truthful. He must be trained to accuracy, or all his ingenuousness will not save him from saying many a thing which is not true. Dr. Johnson advised that if a child said he saw a thing out of one window, when in fact he saw it out of another, he should be set right. I think the Dr. was right; and that a child should consider no kind of misstatement a trifle, seeing always that the parents do not. An open-hearted and ingenuous child is likely to be a great talker; and is in that way more liable to inaccuracy of statement than a reserved child. Oh! let his parents guard him well, by making him early the guardian of the "unruly little member" which may, by neglect, deprive him of the security and peace which should naturally spread from his innocent heart through his open and honest life! Let them help him to add perfect truth of speech to his native truth of heart, and their promising child cannot but be a happy man.

It may seem wearisome to say so often over that the example of the parents is the chief influence in the training of the child; but how can I help saying it when the fact is so? Is it not true that when the father of a family comes home and talks before his children, every word sinks into their minds? If he talks banter—banter so broad that his elder children laugh and understand, how should the little one on its mother's lap fail to be perplexed and misled? It knows nothing about banter, and it looks up seriously in its father's face, and believes all he says, and carries away all manner of absurd ideas. Or, if told not to believe what he hears, how is he to know henceforth what to believe; and how can he put trust in his father's words? The turn for exaggeration which many people have is morally bad for the whole family. It is only the youngest perhaps who will believe that "it rains cats and dogs" because somebody says so; but a whole family may be misled by habitual exaggeration of statement. The consequence is clear. Either they will take up the habit, from imitation of father or mother, or they will learn to distrust their fluent parent. But how safe is everything made by that established habit of truth in a household which acts like an instinct! If the parents are, as by a natural necessity, always accurate in what they say, or, if mistaken, thankful to be set right, and eager to rectify their mistake, the children thrive in an atmosphere of such sincerity and truth: and any one of them to whom truthfulness may be constitutionally difficult, has the best chance for the strengthening of his weakness. Such an one must have sunk under the least aggravation of his infirmity by the sin of his parents: and the probability is, that the whole household would have gone down into moral ruin together; for it cannot be expected that any natural aptitude for truth in children should improve, or even continue, if discouraged by the example of the parents who ought to hail it as a blessing upon their house.

Of all happy households, that is the happiest, where falsehood is never thought of. All peace is broken up when once it appears that there is a liar in the house. All comfort is gone, when suspicion has once entered; when there must be reserve in talk, and reservation in belief. Anxious parents, who are aware of the pains of suspicion, will place generous confidence in their children, and receive what they say freely, unless there is strong reason to distrust the truth of any one. If such an occasion should unhappily arise, they must keep the suspicion from spreading as long as possible; and avoid disgracing their poor child, while there is any chance of his cure by their confidential assistance. He should have their pity and assiduous help, as if he were suffering under some disgusting bodily disorder. If he can be cured, he will become duly grateful for the treatment. If the endeavour fails, means must of course be taken to prevent his example doing harm: and then, as I said, the family peace is broken up, because the family confidence is gone.

I fear that, from some cause or another, there are but few large families where every member is altogether truthful. Some who are not morally guilty, are intellectually incapable of accuracy. But where all are so organised and so trained as to be wholly reliable, in act and word, they are a light to all eyes, and a joy to all hearts. They are a public benefit; for they are a point of general reliance: and they are privately blessed, within and without. Without, their life is made easy by universal trust: and within their home and their hearts, they have the security of rectitude, and the gladness of innocence. If we do but invoke wisdom, she will come, and multiply such homes in our land.

# CHAPTER XVII.

## CONSCIENTIOUSNESS.

We come now to the greatest and noblest of the Moral Powers of Man; to that power which makes him quite a different order of being from any other that we know of, and which is the glory and crown of his existence:—his Conscientiousness. The universal endowment of men with this power is the true bond of brotherhood of the human race. Any race of beings who possess in common the highest quality of which any of them are capable, are brothers, however much they may differ in all other respects, and however little some of them may care about this brotherhood. For those who do care about it, how clear it is, and how very interesting to trace! How plain it is that while men in different parts and ages of the world differ widely as to what is right, they all have something in them which prompts them to do what they believe to be right! Here is a little boy, permitted to try what he can get by selling five shillings' worth of oranges:—he points out to the lady who is buying his last half dozen, that two of them are spotted.—There was Regulus, the Roman general, who was taken prisoner by the enemy, the Carthaginians. He was trusted to go to Rome, to treat for an exchange of prisoners, on his promise that he would return to Carthage,—which he knew was returning to death,—if the Roman senate would not grant an exchange of prisoners. He persuaded the Roman senate not to agree to the exchange, which he believed would not be for the advantage of Rome: and then he went back to Carthage and to death. There is, at this day, the South Sea Islander,—the young wife who has been told that it is pious and right to give her first child to the gods. She has in her all a mother's feelings, all the love which women long to lavish on their first babe: but she desires that the infant should be strangled as soon as born, because she thinks it her duty. Now, this poor creature is truly the sister of the other two, though her superstition is horrible, and the infanticide it leads to is a great crime. She is shockingly ignorant, and her mind is not of that high order which would perceive that there must be something wrong in going against nature in this way: but, for all that, she is conscientious; and by her conscientiousness she is truly a sister in heart to the honourable Roman general, and the honest orange-seller. What she needs is knowledge: and what the whole human race wants is knowledge, to bring the workings of this great power into harmony all over the world. At present, we see men in one place feeding, and in another place burning one another,—because they think they ought. In one place, we see a man with seventy wives,—in another, a man with one wife,—and in another, a man remaining a bachelor all his life; and each one equally supposing that he is doing what is right. The evil everywhere is in the want of clear views of what is right. This is an evil which may and will be remedied, we may hope, in course of ages. There is nothing that we may not hope while the power to desire and do what is right is common to all mankind,—is given to them as an essential part of the human frame.

It does not follow, of course, that this power is equal in all. All but idiots have it, more or less; but it varies, in different individuals, quite as much as any other power. No power is more dependant on care and cultivation for its vigour: but none varies more from the very beginning. Some of the worst cases of want of rectitude that I have known have been in persons so placed as that everybody naturally supposed they must be good, and trusted them accordingly. I have known a girl, brought up by highly principled relatives, in a house where nothing but good was seen or heard of, turn out so faulty as to compel one to see that her power of conscientiousness was the weakest she had. She had some of it. She was uneasy,—truly and not hypocritically,—if she did not read a portion of the bible every day at a certain hour. She was plain, even to prudery, in her dress: she truly honoured old age, and could humble herself before it: and she studiously, and from a sense of duty, administered to the wishes of the elder members of the family, in all matters of arrangement and manners. But that was all. She was tricky to a degree I could never estimate or comprehend. Her little plots and deceptions were without number and without end. Her temper was bad, and she took no pains whatever to mend it, but spent all her exertions in making people as miserable as possible by her vindictiveness. In love matters, she reached a point of malice beyond belief, torturing people's feelings, and getting them into scrapes, with a gratification to her own bad mind which could not be concealed under her demure solemnity of manner. Enough of her! I will only observe that, though she was brought up by good people, it does not follow that she was judiciously managed. The result shows that she was not. A perfectly wise guardian would have seen that her faculty of conscientiousness wanted strengthening, and would have found safe and innocent employment for those powers of secretiveness and defiance, and that inordinate love of approbation, which, as it was, issued in mischief-making.—The opposite case to hers is that which touches one with a deeper pity than almost any spectacle which can be seen on this earth: that of the child whose strong power of conscientiousness is directed to wickedness, before it has ability to help itself. Think of the little child born in a cellar, among thieves! It is born full of human powers; and among these, it has a conscience, and perhaps a particularly strong one. Suppose it is brought up to believe that its duty is to provide money for its parents by stealing. Suppose that, by five years old, it entirely believes that the most wrong thing it can do is to come home at dark without having stolen at least three pocket-handkerchiefs! Such cases have been known; and not a few of them.—And it is only an exaggerated instance of what we very commonly see in history and the world. The Chief Inquisitor in Spain or Italy really believed that he was doing his duty in burning the bodies of heretics for the good of their souls. Our ancestors thought they were acting benevolently in putting badge dresses on charity children. The Pharisees of old were sincere in their belief that it was wrong to heal a sick man on the Sabbath. And I have no doubt that in a future age it will appear that we ourselves are ignorant and mistaken about some points of our conduct in which we now sincerely believe that we are doing what we ought.

In every household, then, the first consideration is to cherish the faculty of conscientiousness; and the next is, to direct it wisely.

When I speak of cherishing the faculty, I do not mean that it is always to be stimulated, whether it be naturally strong or weak. There are cases, and they are not few, where the power is stronger than perhaps any other. In such cases, no stimulating is required, but only guidance and enlightenment. There are few sadder spectacles than that of a suffering being whose conscience has become so tender as to be superstitious; who lives a life of fear—of incessant fear of doing wrong. It is a healthy conscience that we want to produce; a conscience which shall act naturally, vigorously, and incessantly, like an instinct; so as to leave all the other faculties to act freely, without continual conflict and question whether their action be right or wrong. A child who is perpetually driven to examine all he thinks and does will become full of himself, prone to discontent with himself, and to servile dependence on the opinion of those whom he thinks wiser than himself. What is such a child to do when he comes out into the world, and must guide himself? At best, he will go trembling through life, without courage or self-respect: and something worse is to be apprehended. It is to be apprehended that if he makes any slip—and such an one will be sure to think that he does make slips—he will be unable to bear the pain and uncertainty, and will grow reckless. A clergyman, of wide and deep experience, who was the depository of much confidence, told me once (and I have never forgotten it), that some of the worst cases of desperate vice he had ever known were those of young men tenderly and piously reared, who came out from home anxious about the moral dangers of the world and the fears of their parents, and who, having fallen into the slightest fault, and being utterly wretched in consequence, lost all courage and hope, and drowned their misery in indulgence of the worst part of themselves. He felt this so strongly that he solemnly conjured me to use any influence I might ever have over parents in encouraging them to trust their children with their innocence, and to have faith in the best faculties of human nature. This entreaty still rings in my ears, and leads me so to use any influence I may now have over parents.

Is it not true that the strongest delight the human being ever has is in well-doing? Is it not true that this pleasure, like the pleasures of the eye and ear, the pleasures of benevolence, the pleasures of the understanding and the imagination, will seek its own continuance and gratification, if it have fair play? Is it not true that pain of conscience is the worst of human sufferings? and that this pain will be naturally avoided, like every other pain, if only the faculty have fair play?

The worst of it is, the faculty seldom has fair play. The fatal notion that human beings are more prone to evil than inclined to good, and the fatal practice of creating factitious sins, are dreadfully in the way of natural health of conscience. Teach a child that his nature is evil, and you will make it evil. Teach him to fear and despise himself, and you will make him timid and suspicious. Impose upon him a number of factitious considerations of duty, and you will perplex his moral sense, and make him tired of a self-government which has no certainty and no satisfaction in it. It is a far safer and higher way to trust to his natural moral sense, and cultivate his moral taste: to let him grow morally strong by leaving him morally free, and to make him, by sympathy and example, in love with whatever things are pure, honest, and lovely. What the parent has to do with is the moral habits of the child, and not to meddle with his faculties. Give them fair scope to grow, and they will flourish: and, let it be remembered, man has no faculties which are, in themselves and altogether, evil. His faculties are all good, if they are well harmonised. Instead of talking to him, or leading him to talk in his infancy of his own feelings as something that he has to take charge of, fix his mind on the things from which his feelings will of themselves arise. By all means, lead him to be considerate: but not about his own state, but rather about the objects which cause that state. If he sees at home integrity entering into every act and thought, and trust and love naturally ensuing, he will enjoy integrity and live in it, as the native of a southern climate enjoys sunshine and lives in it. If, as must happen, failure of integrity comes under his notice in one direction or another, he will see the genuine disgust and pain which those about him feel at the spectacle, and dishonesty will be disgusting and painful to him. And so on, through all good and bad qualities of men. And this will keep him upright and pure far more certainly than any warnings from you that he will be dishonest and impure, unless he is constantly watching his feelings, and striving against the danger.

In the beginning of his course, he must be aided,—in the early days when the action of all his faculties is weak and uncertain: and this aid cannot be given too early; for we are not aware of any age at which a child has not some sense of moral right and wrong. Mrs. Wesley taught her infants in arms to "cry softly." Without admiring the discipline, we may profit by the hint as to the moral capability of the child. When no older than this, he may have satisfaction, without knowing why, from submitting quietly to be washed, and to go to bed. When he becomes capable of employing himself purposely, he may have satisfaction in doing his business before he goes to his play, and a sense of uneasiness in omitting the duty. I knew a little boy in petticoats who had no particular taste for the alphabet, but began to learn it as a matter of course, without any pretence of relish. One day his lesson was, for some reason, rather short. His conscience was not satisfied. When his elder brother was dismissed, Willie brought his letters again, but found he was not wanted, and might play. The little fellow sighed; and then a bright thought struck him. (I think I see him now, in his white frock, with his large thoughtful eyes lighting up!) He said joyfully—"Willie say his lesson to hisself." He carried his little stool into a corner, put his book on his knees, and finished by honestly covering up the large letters with both hands, and saying aloud two or three new ones. Then he went to his play, all the merrier for the discharge of his conscience.

There is no reason why it should not be thus with all the duties of a child. The great point is that he should see that the peace and joy of the household depend on ease of conscience. His father takes no pleasure till his work is done, and tells the truth to his hurt. His mother seeks to be just to a slandered neighbour, or leaves her rest by the fireside to aid a sick one. Granny's eyes sparkle, or a flush comes over her withered cheek, when she tells the children what good men have endured rather than pretend what they did not believe, or betray a trust. The maid has taken twopence too much in change, and is uneasy till she has returned it, or she refuses to promise something, lest she should be unable to keep her word. His elder sister refuses something good at a neighbour's, because her mother would think it unwholesome while she is not quite well. His elder brother asks him to throw just a little cold water upon him in the mornings, because he is so terribly sleepy that he cannot get up without. And he sees what a welcome is given to a very poor acquaintance, and he feels his own heart beat with reverence for this very poor neighbour, because his father happens to know that the man refused five pounds for his vote at the last election. If the child is surrounded by a moral atmosphere like this, he will derive a strong moral life from it, and a satisfaction to his highest moral faculties which it is scarcely possible that he should forego for the pleasures of sin. The indolent child will, in such a home, lose all idea of pleasure in being idle, and soon find no pleasure till his work is done. The slovenly child will become uneasy under a dirty skin, and the thoughtless one in being behind his time. Common integrity we may suppose to be a matter of course in a household like this; and, as every virtuous faculty naturally advances "from strength to strength," we may hope that the abode will be blessed, as the children grow up, with a very uncommon integrity.

Though the parent will avoid making the child unnecessarily conscious of its own conscience, she (for this is chiefly the mother's business) will remember that her child has his difficulties and perplexities about the working of this, as of all his other imperfectly trained powers; and she will lay herself open to his confidence. Sometimes he is not clear what he ought to do: sometimes he feels himself too weak to do it: sometimes he is miserable because he has done wrong: and then again, he and some one else may differ as to whether he has done wrong or right. And again, he may have seen something in other people's conduct which shocks, or puzzles, or delights him. Oh! let the mother throw open her heart to confidences like these! Let her be sure that the moments of such confidence are golden moments, for which a mother may be more thankful than for anything else she can ever receive from her child. Let it be her care that every child has opportunity to speak freely and privately to her of such things. Some mothers make it a practice to go themselves to fetch the candle when the children are in bed; and then, if wanted, they stay a few minutes, and hear any confessions, or difficulties, and receive any disclosures, of which the little mind may wish to disburden itself before the hour of sleep. Whether then or at another time, it is well worth pondering what a few minutes of serious consultation may do in enlightening and rousing or calming the conscience,—in rectifying and cherishing the moral life. It may be owing to such moments as these that humiliation is raised into humility, apathy into moral enterprise, pride into awe, and scornful blame into Christian pity. Happy is the mother who can use such moments as she ought!

There remains, after all, the dread and wonder what such children are to think and do when they must come to know what is the average conscientiousness of the world. This is a subject of fear and pain to most good parents. But they must consider that their children will not see the world as they do all at once:—not till they have learned, like their parents, to allow for, and account for, what happens in the world. The innocent and the upright put a good construction on as much as possible of what they see; and are often more right in this than their clearer-sighted elders who know more of the tendencies of things. The shock will not come all at once. They hear now of broken contracts, dishonest bargains, venal elections, mercenary marriages, and, perhaps, profligate seductions. They know that there are drunkards, and cheats, and hypocrites, and cruel brutes, in society: and these things hardly affect them, are hardly received by them, because they are surrounded by honest people, and cannot feel what is beyond. And when they must become more truly aware of these things, they will still trust in and admire some whom they look up to, with more or less reason. The knowledge of iniquity will come to them gradually, and all the more safely the less sympathy they have with it.

If it be the pain, and not the danger, of this knowledge that the parents dread, they must make up their minds to it for their children. Surely they do not expect them to go through life without pain: and a bitter suffering it will be to them to see what wretchedness is in the world through the vices and ignorance of men; through their want of conscientiousness, or their errors of conscience. Such pain must be met and endured; and who is likely to meet it so bravely, and endure it so hopefully, as those who are fully aware that every man's heaven or hell is within him—giving a hope that heaven will expand as wisdom grows—and who carry within themselves that peace which the world "can neither give nor take away?"

# CHAPTER XVIII.

## INTELLECTUAL TRAINING.—ITS REQUISITES.

We are all accustomed to speak of the Intellect and moral powers of man as if they were so distinct from one another that we can deal with each set of powers without touching the other.

It is true that there is a division between the intellectual and moral powers of man, as there is between one moral power and another. It is true that we can think of them separately, and treat them separately: but it does not follow that they will work separately. No part of the brain will act alone, no part begins its own action. It is always put in action by another part previously at work, and it excites in its turn some other portion. While we sleep, that part of the brain is at work on which depend those animal functions which are always going on: and, as we know by our dreams, other portions work with this, giving us ideas and feelings during sleep—perhaps as many as by day, if we could only recollect them. The animal portions of the brain set the intellectual and moral organs to work, and these act upon each other, so that there is no separating their action,—no possibility of employing one faculty at a time without help from any other. As memory cannot act till attention has been awakened,—in other words, as people cannot remember what they have never observed and received, so the timid cannot understand, unless it is in a docile and calm state; nor meditate well without the exercise of candour and truthfulness; nor imagine nobly without the help of veneration and hope. If we take any great intellectual work and examine it, we shall see what a variety of faculties, moral as well as intellectual, have gone to the making of it. Take "Paradise Lost," a work so glorious for the loftiness of its imagination, and the extent of its learning, and the beauty of its illustrations, and the harmony of its versification! These are its intellectual beauties: but look what moral beauties are inseparable from these. Look at the veneration,—not only towards God, but towards all holiness, and power, and beauty! Look at the purity, the love, the hopefulness, the strain of high honour throughout! And this intellectual and moral beauty are so blended, that we see how impossible it would be for the one to exist without the other. It is just so in the human character—the intellect of a human being cannot be of a high order, (though some particular faculties may be very strong) if the moral nature is low and feeble: and the moral state cannot be a lofty one where the intellect is torpid.

It does not follow from this that to be very good a child must be exceedingly clever and "highly educated," as we call it. There are plenty of highly-educated people who are not morally good; and there are many honest and amiable and industrious people who cannot read and write. The thing is, we misuse the word "Education." Book-learning is compatible with great poverty of intellect; and there may be a very fine understanding, great power of attention and observation, and possibly, though rarely, of reflection, in a person who has never learned to read,—if the moral goodness of that person has put his mind into a calm and teachable and happy state, and his powers of thought have been stimulated by active affections; if, as we say, his heart has quickened his head. These are truths very important to know; and they ought to be consolatory to parents who are grieved and alarmed because they cannot send their children to school,—supposing that their intellectual part must suffer and go to waste for want of school training and instruction from books. I will say simply and openly what I think about this.

I think that no children, in any rank of life, can acquire so much book-knowledge at home as at a good school, or have their intellectual faculties so well roused and trained. I have never seen an instance of such high attainment in languages, mathematics, history, or philosophy in young people taught at home,—even by the best masters,—as in those who have been in a good school. Without going into the reasons of this, which would lend us out of our way here, I would fully admit the fact.

There are two ways of taking it. First, it cannot be helped. A much larger number of people are unable to send their children to school than can do so. The queen cannot send her children to school: and the children of the peerage are under great disadvantage. The girls cannot, or do not, go from home; and the boys go only to one or another of a very small choice of public schools, where they must run tremendous risks to both morals and intellect. Then there are multitudes of families, in town and country, among rich and poor, where the children must be taught at home. The number is much larger of the children who do not go to school than of those who do. If we consider, again, how large a proportion of schools, taking them from the highest to the lowest, are so bad that children learn little in them, it is clear that the home-trained intellects are out of all proportion more numerous than the school-trained.

The other way of looking at the matter is in order to inquire what school advantages may be brought home—what there is in the school that children may have the benefit of at home.

The fundamental difference between school and home is clear enough. At school, everything is done by rule; by a law which was made without a view to any particular child, and which governs all alike: whereas, at home, the government is not one of law, working on from year to year without change, but of love, or, at least, of the mind of the parents, varying with circumstances, and with the ages and dispositions of the children. There is no occasion to point out here how great are the moral advantages of a good home in comparison with the best of schools. Our business now is with the intellectual training. Can the advantages of school law be brought into the home?

I think they may, to a certain extent: and I think it of great importance that they should. Law will not do all at home that it does at school. It is known to be new made, for the sake of the parties under it; and it cannot possibly work so undeviatingly in a family as in a school; and the children of a family, no two of whom are of the same age, cannot have their faculties so stimulated to achieve irksome labour as in a large class of comrades of the same age and standing. But still, rule and regularity will do much: and when we consider the amount of drudgery that children have to get through in acquiring the elements of knowledge, we shall feel it to be only humane and fair to give them any aid that can be afforded through the plans of the household.

Those kinds and parts of knowledge which interest the reasoning faculties and the imagination are not in question just now. They come by and by, and can better take care of themselves, or are more sure to be taken care of by others, than the drudgery which is the first stage in all learning. The drudgery comes first; and it is wise and kind to let it come soon enough. The quickness of eye, and tenacity and readiness of memory, which belong to infancy should be made use of while at their brightest, for gaining such knowledge as is to be had by the mere eye, ear, and memory. How easily can the most ordinary child learn a hymn or other piece of poetry by heart;—sometimes before it can speak plain, and very often indeed before it can understand the meaning! What a pity that this readiness should not be used,—that the child, for instance, should not learn to count, and to read, and to say the multiplication table, while it can learn these things with the least trouble! We must remember that while we see the child to be about a great and heavy work, the child himself does not know this, and cannot be oppressed by the thought. All he knows about is the little bit he learns every day. And that little bit is easy to him, if the support of law be given him. It is here that law must come in to help him. He should, if possible, be saved all uncertainty, all conflict in his little mind, as to his daily business. If there is a want of certainty and punctuality about his lessons, there will be room for the thought of something which, for the moment, he would like better; and again, his young faculties will become confused and irregular in their working from uncertainty of seasons and of plans. If there can be a particular place, and a particular time for him, every day but Sundays, and he is never put off, his faculties will come to their work with a freshness and steadiness which nothing but habit will secure. A law of work which leaves him no choice, but sets all his faculties free for his business, saves him half the labour of it; as it does in after life to those who are so blessed as to be destined to necessary, and not voluntary labour. In houses where there cannot be a room set apart for the lessons, perhaps there may be a corner. If there cannot be any place, perhaps there may be a time: and the time should be that which can best be secured from interruption. Where the father is so fond of his children, and so capable of self-denial for their sakes as to devote an hour or two of his evenings to the instruction of his children, he may rely upon it that he is heaping up blessings for himself with every minute of those hours. His presence, the presence of the worker of the household, is equal to school and home influence together. The scantiness of his leisure makes the law; and his devotedness in using it thus makes the inestimable home influence. Under his teaching, if it be regular and intelligent, head and heart will come on together, to his encouragement now, and his great future satisfaction.

When I come to speak of habits, by and by, it will be seen that this introduction of law at home is to relate only to affairs of habit, and intellectual attainment. The misfortune of school is that the affections and feelings must come under the control of law, instead of the guidance of domestic love. It would be a wanton mischief indeed to spoil the freedom of home by stretching rule and law there beyond their proper province.

There are houses, many houses, and not always very poor ones, where the parents think they cannot provide for the intellectual improvement of their children, and mourn daily over the thought. I wish such parents could be induced to consider well what intellectual improvement is, and then they would see how much they may do for their children's minds without book, pen, or paper. It goes against me to suppose children brought up without knowledge of reading and writing; and I trust this is not likely to be the fate of any children of the parents who read this. But it is as well to suppose the extreme case, in order to see whether even people who cannot read and write must remain ignorant and debarred from the privileges of mind.

In America I saw many families of settlers, where the children were strangely circumstanced. There was always plenty to eat and drink; the barns were full of produce, and there were horses in the meadow; and every child would have hereafter a goodly portion of land: but there were no servants, and there could be no "education," because the mother and children had to do all the work of the house. In one of these homes the day was spent thus.—The father (a man of great property) went out upon his land, before daylight, taking with him his little sons of six and seven years old, who earned their breakfasts by leading the horses down to water, and turning out the cows, and sweeping the stable: and, when the milking was done (by a man on the farm, I think), they brought up the milk. Meantime, their mother, an educated English lady, took up the younger children, and swept the kitchen, lighted the fire, and cooked the beef-steak for her husband's breakfast, and boiled the eggs which the little ones brought in from the paddock. Soon after seven, the farmer and boys were gone again: and then the mother set down in the middle of the kitchen floor a large bowl of hot water and the breakfast things: and the little girl of four, and her sister of two, set to work. The elder washed the cups and dishes, and the younger wiped them, as carefully and delicately as if she had been ten years older. She never broke anything, or failed to make all bright and dry. Then they went to make their own little beds: they could just manage that, but not the larger ones. Meantime, their mother was baking, or washing, or brewing, or making soap,—boiling it in a cauldron over a fire in the wood. There were no grocers' shops within scores of miles. In the season, the family had to make sugar in the forest from their maple trees; and wine from the fruit they grew: and there were the apples, in immense quantities, to be split and cored, and hung up in strings for winter use. Every morning in the week was occupied with one or another of these employments; and in the midst of them, dinner had to be cooked, and ready by noon: another beef-steak, with apple-sauce or onions, and hot "corn" bread (made of Indian meal), and a squash pie, or something of the sort. There was enough to do, all the afternoon, in finishing off the morning's work: and there must be another steak for tea or supper.— The children had been helping all day: and now their parents wished to devote this time,—after six p.m.—to their benefit. It is true, the mother had now to sew; this being her only time for making and mending: but she got out the slates and lesson-books, and put one little girl and boy before her, while their father took the other two, and set them a sum and a copy on the slate. But alas! by this time, no one of the party could keep awake. They did try. The parents were so extremely anxious for their children that they did strive: but nature was overpowered. After a few struggles, the children were sent to bed; and in the very midst of a sentence, the mother's head would sink over her work, and the father's down upon the table, in irresistible sleep. Both had been very fond of chess, in former days: and the husband bade his wife put away her work, and try a game of chess. But down went the board, and off slid the men, in the middle of a game! Now,—what could be done for the children's education here? In time, there was hope that roads and markets would be opened where the produce of the farm might be sold, and money obtained to send the children to schools, some hundreds of miles off: or, at least, that neighbours enough might settle round about to enable the township to invite a school-master. But what could be done meantime?

So much might be, and was, done as would astonish people who think that intellectual education means school learning. I do not at all wish to extenuate the misfortune of these children in being doomed to write a bad hand, if any; to be slow at accounts; to have probably no taste for reading; and no knowledge, except by hearsay, of the treasures of literature. But I do say that they were not likely to grow up ignorant and stupid. They knew every tree in the forest, and every bird, and every weed. They knew the habits of all domestic animals. They could tell at a glance how many scores of pigeons there were in a flock, when clouds of these birds came sailing towards the wood. They did not want to measure distances, for they knew them by the eye. They could give their minds earnestly to what they were about; and ponder, and plan, and imagine, and contrive. Their faculties were all awake. And they obtained snatches of stories from father and mother, about the heroes of old times, and the history of England and America. They worshipped God, and loved Christ, and were familiar with the Bible. Now, there are some things here that very highly educated people among us might be glad to be equal to: and the very busiest father, the hardest-driven mother in England may be able, in the course of daily business, to rouse and employ the faculties of their children,—their attention, understanding, reflection, memory and imagination,—so as to make their intellects worth more than those of many children who are successful at school. Their chance is doubled if books are opened to them: but if not, there is nothing to despair about.

I was much struck by a day's intellectual education of a little boy of seven who was thrown out of his usual course of study and play. The family were in the country,—in a house which they had to themselves for a month, in beautiful scenery, where they expected to be so continually out of doors that the children's toys were left at home. Some days of unintermitting, drenching rain came; and on one of these days, the little fellow looked round him, after breakfast, and said, "Papa, I don't exactly see what I can do." He would have been thankful to say his lessons: but papa was absolutely obliged to write the whole day; and mama was up-stairs nursing his little sister, who had met with an accident. His papa knew well how to make him happy. He set him to find out the area of the house, and of every room in it. He lent him a three-foot rule, showed him how he might find the thickness of the walls, and gave him a slate and pencil. This was enough. All day, he troubled nobody, but went quietly about, measuring and calculating, and writing down;—from morning till dinner,—from dinner till supper: and by that time he had done. When they could go out to measure the outside, they found him right to an inch: and the same with every room in the house.— This boy was no genius. He was an earnest, well-trained boy: and who does not see that if he and his parents had lived in an American forest, or in the severest poverty at home, he would have been, in the best sense, an educated boy! He would not have understood several languages, as he does now: but his faculties would have been busy and cultivated, if he had never in his life seen any book but the Bible.—Anxious parents may take comfort from the thought that nothing ever exists or occurs which may not be made matter of instruction to the mind of man. The mind and the material being furnished to the parents' hands, it is their business to bring them together, whether books be among the material or not.

# CHAPTER XIX.

## INTELLECTUAL TRAINING. ORDER OF DEVELOPMENT. THE PERCEPTIVE FACULTIES.

In beginning a child's intellectual education, the parent must constantly remember to carry on his care of the frame, spoken of in a former chapter. The most irritable and tender part of a child's frame is its brain; and on the welfare of its brain every thing else depends. It should not be forgotten that the little creature was born with a soft head; and that it takes years for the contents of that skull to become completely guarded by the external bones, and sufficiently grown and strengthened to bear much stress. Nature points out what the infant's brain requires, and what it can bear; and if the parents are able to discern and follow the leadings of nature, all will be well. The most certain thing is that there is no safety in any other course.

In their anxiety to bring up any lagging faculty,—to cherish any weak power,—parents are apt to suppose those faculties weak, for whose development they are looking too soon. It grieves me to see conscientious parents, who govern their own lives by reasoning, stimulating a young child to reason long before the proper time. The reflective and reasoning faculties are among the last that should naturally come into use; and the only safe way is to watch for their first activity, and then let it have scope. One of the finest children I ever saw,—a stout handsome boy, with a full set of vigorous faculties, was, at five years old, in danger of being spoiled in a strange sort of way. The process was stopped in time to save his intellect and his morals; but not before it had strewn his youthful life with difficulties from which he need never have suffered. This boy heard a great deal of reasoning always going on; and he seldom or never saw any children, except in parties, or in the street. His natural imitation of the talk of grown up people was encouraged; and from the time he could speak, he saw in the whole world,—in all the objects that met his senses,—only things to reason about. He gathered flowers, not so much because he liked them as because they might be discoursed about. He could not shut the door, or put on his pinafore when bid, till the matter was argued, and the desired act proved to be reasonable. The check was, as I have said, given in time: but he had much to do to bring up his perceptive faculties and his mechanical habits to the point required in even a decent education. He had infinite trouble in learning to spell, and in mastering all the elements of knowledge which are acquired by the memory: and his writing a good hand, and being ready at figures, or apt at learning a modern language by the ear, was hopeless. He would doubtless have done all these well, if his faculties had been exercised in their proper order;—that is, in the order which nature indicates,—and vindicates.

And now,—what is that order?

The Perceptive faculties come first, into activity. Do we not all remember that colours gave us more intense pleasure in our early childhood than they have ever done since? Most of us can remember back to the time when we were four years old,—or three; and some even two. What is it that we remember? With one, it is a piece of gay silk, or printed cotton or china; or a bed of crocuses;—or we remember the feel of a piece of velvet or fur, or something rough;—or the particular shape of some leaf;—or the amazing weight of a globule of quicksilver;—or the immense distance from one end of the room to the other. I, for one, remember several things that happened when I was between two and three years old: and most of these were sensations, exciting passions. I doubt whether I ever felt keener delight than in passing my fingers round a flat button, covered with black velvet, on the top of a sister's bonnet. I remember lighting upon the sensation, if one may say so; and the intense desire afterwards to be feeling the button. And just at that time I was sent into the country for my health; and I can now tell things about the first day in the cottage which no one can ever have told to me. I tried to walk round a tree (an elm, I believe), clasping the tree with both arms: and nothing that has happened to-day is more vivid to me than the feel of the rough bark to the palms of my hands, and the entanglement of the grass to my feet. And then at night there was the fearful wonder at the feel of the coarse calico sheets, and at the creaking of the turn-up bedstead when I moved.—After I came home, when I was two years and nine months old, I saw, one day, the door of the spare bed-room ajar, and I pushed it open and went in. I was walking about the house because I had a pair of new shoes on, and I liked to hear their pit-pat, and to make sure that I could walk in them, though they were slippery. The floor of the spareroom was smooth and somewhat polished; and it was—(at least to my eyes—) a large room. I was half-frightened when I saw that the blinds were down. But there was a fire; and standing by the fire, at the further end, was an old woman—(or to me she looked old)—with a muslin handkerchief crossed over her gown: and in her arms she held a bundle of flannel. The curtains of the bed were drawn;—the fawn-coloured moreen curtains with a black velvet edge, which I sometimes stroked for a treat. The old woman beckoned to me; and I wished to go; but I thought I could never walk all that way on the polished floor without a tumble. I remember how wide I stretched out my arms, and how far apart I set my feet, and how I got to the old woman at last. With her foot she pushed forwards a tiny chair, used as a footstool, embroidered over with sprawling green leaves; and there I sat down: and the old woman laid the bundle of flannel across my lap. With one hand she held it there safe, and with the other she uncovered the little red face of a baby. Though the sight set every pulse in my body beating, I do not remember feeling any fear,—though I was always afraid of everything. It was a passionate feeling of wonder, and a sort of tender delight;—delight at being noticed and having it on my lap, perhaps, as much as at the thing itself. How it ended, I do not know. I only remember further seeing with amazement, that somebody was in the bed,—that there was a nightcap on the pillow,—though it was day-time. These details may seem trifling: but, if we want to know what faculties are vigorous in infancy, it is as well to learn, in any way we can, what children feel and think at the earliest age we can arrive at. One other instance of vivid perception stands out among many in my childhood so remarkably as to be perhaps instructive: and the more so because I was not endowed with quick senses, or strong perceptive powers, but, on the contrary, discouraged my teachers by dullness and inattention, and a constant tendency to reverie. I was always considered a remarkably unobservant child.

I slept with the nursemaid in a room at the top of the house which looked eastwards: and the baby brother mentioned above, now just able to walk, slept in a crib by the bedside. One summer morning I happened to wake before sunrise, and thought it very strange to see the maid asleep; the next thing I remember was walking over the boards with bare feet, and seeing some little pink toes peeping out through the rails of the crib. I gently pinched them, and somehow managed to keep the child quiet when he reared himself up from his pillow; he must have caught some of the spirit of the prank, for he made no noise. I helped him to scramble down from the crib, and led him to the window, and helped him to scramble upon a chair: and then I got up beside him; and, by using all my strength, I opened the window. How chill the air was! and how hard and sharp the window-sill felt to my arms! We were so high above the street that I dared not look down; but oh! what a sight we saw by looking abroad over the tops of the houses to the rising ground beyond! The sun must have been coming up, for the night-clouds were of the richest purple, turning to crimson; and in one part there seemed to be a solid edge of gold. I have seen the morning and evening skies of all the four quarters of the world, but this is, in my memory, the most gorgeous of all, though it could not in fact have been so. I whispered all I knew about God making the sun come up every morning; and I certainly supposed the child to sympathise with me in the thrilling awe of the moment: but it could not have been so. I have some remembrance of the horrible difficulty of getting the window down again, and of hoisting up my companion into his crib: and I can distinctly recal the feelings of mingled contempt and fear with which I looked upon the maid, who had slept through all this; and how cold my feet were when I crept into bed again.

Now, if this is what children are, it seems plain that the faculties by which they perceive objects so vividly should be simply trained to a good use. The parent has little more to do than to see that Nature is not hindered in her working: to see that the faculties are awake, and that a sufficient variety is offered for them to employ themselves upon. Nothing like what is commonly called teaching is required here, or can do anything but harm at present. If the mother is at work, and the children are running in and out of the garden, it is only saying to the little toddler, "Now bring me a blue flower;—now bring me a yellow flower;—now bring me a green leaf." At another time, she will ask for a round stone; or a thick stick; or a thin stick. And sometimes she will blow a feather, and let it fall again: or she will blow a dandelion-head all to pieces, and quite away. If she is wise, she will let the child alone, to try its own little experiments, and learn for itself what is hard and what is soft; what is heavy and light; hot and cold; and what it can do with its little limbs and quick senses. Taking care, of course, that it does not injure itself, and that it has objects within reach in sufficient variety, she cannot do better, at this season of its life, than let it be busy in its own way. I saw a little fellow, one day, intently occupied for a whole breakfast-time, and some time afterwards, in trying to put the key of the house-door into the key-hole of the tea-caddy. When he gave the matter up, and not before, his mother helped him to see why he could not do it. If she had taken the door-key from him at first, he would have missed a valuable lesson. At this period of existence, the children of rich and poor have, or may have, about equal advantages, under the care of sensible parents. They can be busy about anything. There is nothing that cannot be made a plaything of, and a certain means of knowledge, if the faculties be awake. If the child be dull, it must, of course, be tempted to play. If the faculties be in their natural state of liveliness, the mother has only to be aware that the little creature must be busy while it is awake, and to see that it has variety enough of things (the simpler the better) to handle, and look at, and listen to, and experiment upon.

The perceptive faculties have a relation to other objects than those which are presented to the five senses. It is very well for children to be picking up from day to day knowledge about colours and forms, and the hardness and weight of substances, and the habits of animals, and the growth of plants;—the great story, in short, of what passes before their eyes, and appeals to their ears, and impresses them through the touch: but there is another range of knowledge appropriate to the perceptive faculties. There are many facts that can be perceived through another medium than the eye, the ear, or the hand. Facts of number and quantity, for instance, are perceived (after a time, if not at first) without illustration by objects of sight or sound: and it is right, and kind to the child, to help him to a perception of these facts early, while the perceiving faculties are in their first vigour. There is no hardship in this, if the thing is done in moderation: and in many cases, this exertion of the perceptive faculties is attended with a keen satisfaction. I have known an idiot child, perfectly infantine in his general ways, amuse himself half the day long with employing his perceptions of number and quantity. He, poor child, was incapable of being taught anything as a lesson: he did not understand speech,—beyond a very few words: but the exercise of such faculties as he had—(and the strongest he had were those of Order, and Perception of number, quantity and symmetry) was the happiness of his short and imperfect life: and the exercise of the same faculties,—moderate and natural exercise,—may make part of the happiness of every child's life.

It is very well to use the faculty of eye and ear as an introduction to the use of the inner perceptions,—so to speak. For instance, it is well to teach a child the multiplication-table, by the ear as well as the understanding:—to teach it by rote, (as one teaches a tune without words), as an avenue to the mystery of numbers: but the pleasure to the pupil is in perceiving the relations of numbers. In the same manner, the eye may be used for the same purpose; as when the mother teaches by pins on the table, or by peas, or peppercorns, that two and two make four; and that three fours, or two sixes, or four threes, all make twelve: but the pleasure to the pupil is in perceiving the relations of these numbers without pins or peppercorns,—in the head; and in going on till he has mastered all the numbers in the multiplication-table,—perceiving them in the depths of his mind, without light or sound,—without images or words. Children who are capable of mental arithmetic delight in it, before their minds are tired:—and the moment the mind is tired, the exercise should stop.

About quantity, the same methods may be used. At first, there must be measurement, to prove to the child the relation of quantities: but to what a point of precision the mind may arrive, after having once perceived the truth of quantities and spaces, is seen in the fact that astronomers can infallibly predict eclipses centuries before they happen. Another department of what is called exact knowledge comprehends the relations of time. This is another case in which idiots have proved to us that there is an inner perception of time,—a faculty which works pleasurably when once set to work. One idiot who had lived near a striking clock, and was afterwards removed from all clocks, and did not know a watch by sight, went on to the end of his life imitating the striking of the hour regularly, with as much precision as the sun marks it upon the dial. Another who never had sense enough to know of the existence of clock or watch, could never be deceived about the precise time of day. Under all changes of place and households with their habits, he did and looked for the same things at exactly the same moment of every day. And by this faculty it is that even little children learn the clock;—a process which, from its very nature, could never be learned by rote. In these matters, again, the children of the poor can be as well trained as those of the rich. Every where, and under all circumstances, people can measure and compute. The boy must do it if he is to practise any art or trade whatever; and in every household, there is, or ought to be, enough of economy,—of measuring, and cutting out, and counting and calculating, for the girl to exercise her faculty of perception of number and quantity. The understanding of money is no mean exercise, in itself. In one rank, we see the able builder, carpenter, and mechanician, practised in these departments of perception: and in another we see the astronomer detecting and marking out the courses of the stars, and understanding the mighty mechanism of the heavens, as if he had himself trodden all the pathways of the sky. It is wise and kind to use the early vigour of these faculties—the powers which perceive facts,—up to the limit of satisfaction, stopping short always of fatigue.

This is the season too, and these are the faculties, to be employed in learning by rote. Learning by rote is nothing of a drudgery now compared with what it is afterwards;—for the ear is quick, the eye is free and at liberty; the memory is retentive, and the understanding is not yet pressing for its gratification. At this season too, as has been before observed, the child does not look forward, nor comprehend what it is attempting. The present hour, with its little portion of occupation, is all that it sees: and it accomplishes vast things, bit by bit, which it would never attempt if it knew the sum of the matter. No one would learn to speak if he knew all that speech comprehends: yet every child learns to speak, easily and naturally. Thus it is with every art, every science, every department of action and knowledge. The beginning,—the drudgery—should be got over at the time when it costs least fatigue. And this is why we teach children early to read;—so early that, but for this consideration, it is of no consequence whether they can read or not. We do it while the eye is quick to notice the form of the letters, and while the ear is apt to catch their sound, and before the higher faculties come in with any disturbing considerations. My own opinion is that, on account of the feebleness and uncertainty of the hand, writing had better be taught later than it usually is;—that is, when the child shows an inclination to draw or scribble,—to describe any forms on slate or paper, or on walls or sand. But whatever depends mainly on eye, ear, and memory, should be taught early, when the learning causes the most gratification and the least pain. The help that this arrangement gives to, and receives from, the formation of habits of regularity and industry will come under notice when I speak hereafter of the Care of the Habits.

According to what has been said, a child's first intellectual education lies in varied amusement, without express teaching. This is while its brain is infantine and tender, and its nature restless and altogether sensitive. When it shows itself quieter and more thoughtful, it may be expressly taught, a little at a time, with cheerful steadiness and tender encouragement. What it should learn, a healthy well-trained child will, for the most part, indicate for itself, by its inquiries, and its pleasure in learning. What the parent has to impose upon it is that which, being artificial, it cannot indicate for itself,—the art of reading, and the names and forms of numbers, and such arrangements of language as are found in simple poetry, or other useful forms which may be committed to memory. It is impossible to lay down any rule as to the age to be comprehended in this period; and it might be dangerous to do so;—so various are the capacities and temperaments of children; but, speaking quite indeterminately, I may say that I have had in view the period, for ordinary children, from the opening of the faculties to about seven years old.

## CHAPTER XX.

## INTELLECTUAL TRAINING.—THE CONCEPTIVE FACULTIES.

Up to this point, and for some way beyond it, children are better off at home than at school; and no parent should be induced to think otherwise by what is seen to be achieved at Infant Schools. At some Infant Schools, little children who can scarcely speak, are found able to say and do many wonderful things which might make inexperienced mothers fear that their little ones at home had not been done justice to, and must be sadly backward in their education: but if the anxious mother will consider a little, and keep on the watch, she will perceive that her children are better at home. These Infant Schools were set on foot with the most benevolent of intentions; and they are really a vast benefit to a large class in society: but it does not follow that they afford the best training for infants. In their very nature they cannot do so. When we stand in the midst of such an assemblage, we feel what a blessing it is that little creatures who would be locked up in garrets all day while the parents were at work, liable to falls or fire, or who would be tumbling about in the streets or roads, dirty, quarrelsome, and exposed to bad company, should be collected here under safe guardianship, and taught, and kept clean, and amused with harmless play: but we cannot help seeing, at the same time, that there is something unnatural in the method; and whatever is unnatural is always radically bad. Nature makes households, family groups where no two children are of the same age, and where, with the utmost activity, there is a certain degree of quietness, retirement, and repose; whereas, in the Infant School there is a crowd of little creatures, dozens of whom are of the same age; and quietness can be obtained only by drilling, while play occasions an uproar which no nerves can easily bear. The brain and nerves of infants are tender and irritable; and in the quietest home, a sensible mother takes care that the little creature is protected from hurry, and loud noises, and fear, and fatigue of its faculties. She sees when it begins to look pale, or turns cross or sick, and instantly removes it from excitement. But it is impossible thus to protect each child in a school: and the consequence is that the amount of mortality in Infant Schools, as in every large assemblage of infants, is very great. There is no saying whether as many might not perish from accident and some kind of misery, if they were left in their garrets and street haunts; but the facts show that home is the proper place for little children whose parents make a real home for them; and no apparent forwardness of school infants can alter the case.

In truth, school is no place of education for any children whatever till their minds are well put in action. This is the work which has to be done at home, and which may be done in all homes where the mother is a sensible woman. This done, a good school is a resource of inestimable advantage for cultivating the intellect, and aiding the acquisition of knowledge: but it is of little or no use without preparation at home. So at the age of which we speak, parents may be satisfied that they have the matter in their own hands.

We have seen that the Perceptive faculties are the first of the intellectual powers which act: and that there is plenty of material for their exercise everywhere, and all day long.

The next set of faculties comes pretty early into operation, and so much of the future wealth of the mind depends on their cultivation that they ought to have the serious attention of parents. I refer to the Conceptive faculties. The time has come when the child is perhaps less intensely impressed by actual objects, while it becomes capable of conceiving of something that it does not see. At this period, the little boy drags about the horse that has lost head and tail and a leg or two: and the little girl hugs a rag bundle which she calls her doll. The boy does not want a better horse, nor the girl a real doll. The idea is every thing to them, by virtue of their conceptive faculty. Staring, meagre pictures please them now,—better than the finest; and stories, with few incidents and no filling up. The faculty is so vigorous, while, of course, very narrow in its range, from the scantiness of the child's knowledge, that the merest sketch is enough to stimulate it to action; the rudest toys, the most meagre drawing, the baldest story. The mother's business is now clear and easy. Her business is to supply more and more material for these faculties to work upon:—to give, as occasion arises, more and more knowledge of actual things, and furnish representations or suggestions in the course of her intercourse with the child. Nothing is easier; for in fact she has only to make herself the child's cheerful companion: and in a manner which can go on while she is employed in her household occupations, or walking in the fields or the streets. The child asks a myriad of questions; and she must make some kind of cheerful answer to them all, if she lets him talk at all. She will often have to tell him that she does not know this or that; for a child's questions reach far beyond the bounds of our knowledge: but she must not leave him without some sort of answer to appease his restless faculties. And his questions will suggest to her a multitude of things to tell him which he will be eager to hear, as long as they hang upon any thing real which he knows already. Stories and pictures (including toys, which to him are pictures) are what he likes best; and she will make either stories or pictures,—short and vivid,—of what she tells him. The stories and pictures of her conversation must be simple and literal; and so must any sketches she may make for him with pencil and paper, or a bit of chalk upon the pavement. She may make four straight strokes, with two horizontal lines above, and a circle for a head, and call it a horse; and a horse it will be to him, because it calls up the image of a horse in his mind.

But if she draws it ever so well, and puts wings to it, he will not like it half so much, even if she tells him that its name is Pegasus, and there are some pretty stories about such a horse. Perhaps he will be afraid of it.

There can scarcely be a stronger instance of the power of such a child's conceptive faculty than in his own attempts to draw. He draws the cat, or a soldier, and is in raptures with it. Mark his surprise when his mother points out to him that the cat's head is bigger than her body, and that the soldier is all legs and arms and gun, and has no body at all. He sees this, and admits it, and draws a better one: but he would not have found out for himself that there was anything amiss the first time. The idea was complete in his mind; and he thought he saw its representation on the paper, till his mother roused his perceptive powers by making him observe the real cat and soldier, and their proportions. I remember once being amused at seeing how very short a time was necessary to bring the perceptive faculties into their due relation to the conceptive. A little boy who had taken a journey, was exceedingly delighted with the river-side inn at Ferry-bridge in Yorkshire; and he must draw it. When he was a hundred miles further north, he must draw it again: and diligently enough he persevered, kneeling on a chair,—drawing the river and the bridge, and a house, and a heap of coals,—each coal being round, and almost as big as the house. When his paper was nearly all scrawled over, he went unwillingly away to his dinner, from which he hastened back to his drawing. But O! what consternation there was in his face, and what large tears rolled down his cheeks, till he hid his face with his pinafore. He wailed and sobbed:—"somebody had spoiled his drawing." When asked what made him think so, and assured that nobody had touched it, he sobbed out "I'm sure I never made it such a muddle." Before dinner, he saw his work with the conceptive,—after dinner with the perceptive faculties; and it is no wonder that he thought two persons had been at it.

Without going over again any of the ground traversed in the chapter on Fear, I may just observe that at this period children are particularly liable to fear. Almost any appearance suffices to suggest images; and the repetition of any image invariably, at any time or place, is in itself terrifying to those of older nerves than the children we are thinking of. Now is the time when portraits seem to stare at the gazer, and to turn their eyes wherever he moves. Now is the time when a crack in the plaster of a wall, or an outline in a chintz pattern or a paper-hanging, suggests the image of some monster, and perhaps makes the child afraid of his room or his bed, while his mother has no perception of the fact. The mother should be on the watch, without any appearance of being so.

I have spoken of only the early stage of the activity of the conceptive faculties. We see how it goes on in the appetite for fiction which is common to all children,—in the eagerness of boys for books of voyages and travels, and for playing soldiers, and school-master, and making processions, while the girls are playing school-mistress, and dressing up, and pretending to be the queen. The whole period is, or ought to be, very precious to the parents; for it is the time for storing their children's minds with images and ideas, which are the materials for the exercise of the higher faculties at a later time. The simple method of management is to practise the old maxim "Live and let live." The mother's mind must be awake, to meet the vivacious mind of the child: and she must see that the child's is lively and natural, and be careful neither to over-excite it by her anxiety to be always teaching, nor to baulk and depress it by discouraging too much its sometimes inconvenient loquacity and curiosity. It is well that there should be times when children of six and upwards should amuse themselves and one another without troubling their elders; but a vivacious child must talk and inquire a great deal every day, or, if repressed, suffer from some undue exercise of its mental activity.

It should never be forgotten that the happier a child is, the cleverer he will be. This is not only because, in a state of happiness, the mind is free, and at liberty for the exercise of its faculties, instead of spending its thoughts and energy in brooding over troubles; but also because the action of the brain is stronger when the frame is in a state of hilarity: the ideas are more clear; impressions of outward objects are more vivid; and the memory will not let them slip. This is reason enough for the mother to take some care that she is the cheerful guide and comforter that her child needs. If she is anxious or fatigued she will exercise some control over herself, and speak cheerfully, and try to enter freely into the subject of the moment;—to meet the child's mind, in short, instead of making his sink for want of companionship. A rather low instance of the effect of the stimulus of joy in quickening the powers occurred within my knowledge;—a rather low one, but illustrative enough. A little girl, the youngest of her class at school, did her French lessons fairly; but, as a matter of course, was always at or near the bottom, while a tall girl, five years older, clever and industrious, was always, as a matter of course, at the top. One day, there happened to be a long word in question in the vocabulary, which nobody knew but the little girl; so she went to the top. There was not much excitement of ambition in the case: she felt it to be an accident merely, and the tall girl was very kind to her;—there could hardly be less of the spirit of rivalry in such a case than there was here. But the joy of the child was great; and her surprise,—both at the fact of her position, and at the power she found in herself to keep it;—and keep it she did for many weeks, though the tall girl never missed a word in all that time. The dull French vocabulary suddenly became to the child a book of living imagery. The very letters of the words impressed themselves like pictures upon her memory; and each word, becoming suddenly interesting of itself, called up some imagery, which prevented its being forgotten. All this was pleasant; and then there was the comfort and security about the lesson being perfect. The child not only hoped every day that she should get well through, but felt it impossible that she should ever forget a word of it. When at last she failed, it was through depression of spirits. While she was learning her lesson at home, her baby- sister was ill, and crying sadly. It was impossible to get any impression out of the book:—the page turned into common French vocabulary again; and the next morning, not only the tall girl stepped into her proper place, but the little one rapidly passed down to her old stand at the bottom.

Children who read from the love of reading are usually supremely happy over their book. A wise parent will indulge the love of reading, not only from kindness in permitting the child to do what it likes best, but because what is read with enjoyment has intense effect upon the intellect. The practice of reading for amusement must not begin too soon: and it must be permitted by very slow degrees, till the child is so practised in the art of reading as to have its whole mind at liberty for the subject, without having to think about the lines or the words. Till he is sufficiently practised for this, he should be read to: and it will then soon appear whether he is likely to be moderate when he gets a book into his own hands.—My own opinion is that it is better to leave him to his natural tastes,—to his instincts,—when that important period of his life arrives which makes him an independent reader. Of course, his proper duty must be done;—his lessons, or work of other kinds, and his daily exercise. But it seems to me better to abstain from interfering with that kind of strong inclination than to risk the evils of thwarting it. Perhaps scarcely any person of mature years can conceive what the appetite for reading is to a child. It goes off, or becomes changed in mature years, to such a degree as to make the facts of a reading childhood scarcely credible in remembrance, or even when before the eyes. But it is all right; and the process had better not be disturbed. The apprehension of a child is so quick, his conceptive faculty is so ravenous for facts and pictures, or the merest suggestions, and he is so entirely free from those philosophical checks which retard in adults the process of reception from books, that he can, at ten years old, read the same book twice as fast as he can,—if he duly improves meanwhile,—twenty years later. I have seen a young girl read Moore's Lalla Rookh through, except a very few pages, before breakfast,—and not a late breakfast; and not a passage of the poem was ever forgotten. When she had done, the Arabian scenes appeared to be the reality, and the breakfast table and brothers and sisters the dream: but that was sure to come right; and all the ideas of the thick volume were added to her store. I have seen a school-boy of ten lay himself down, back uppermost, with the quarto edition of "Thalaba" before him, on the first day of the Easter holidays, and turn over the leaves, notwithstanding his inconvenient position, as fast as if he was looking for something, till, in a very few hours it was done, and he was off with it to the public library, bringing back the "Curse of Kehama." Thus he went on with all Southey's poems, and some others, through his short holidays,—scarcely moving voluntarily all those days except to run to the library. He came out of the process so changed, that none of his family could help being struck by it. The expression of his eye, the cast of his countenance, his use of words, and his very gait were changed. In ten days, he had advanced years in intelligence: and I have always thought that this was the turning-point of his life. His parents wisely and kindly let him alone,—aware that school would presently put an end to all excess in the new indulgence. I can speak from experience of what children feel towards parents who mercifully leave them to their own propensities,—forbearing all reproach about the ill manners and the selfishness of which the sinners are keenly conscious all the while. Some children's greediness for books is like a drunkard's for wine. They can no more keep their hands off a beloved book than the tippler from the bottle before him. The great difference as to the safety of the case is that the child's greediness is sure to subside into moderation in time, from the development of new faculties, while the drunkard's is sure to go on increasing till all is over with him. If parents would regard the matter in this way, they would neither be annoyed at the excess of the inconvenient propensity, nor proud of any child who has it. It is no sign yet of a superiority of intellect; much less of that wisdom which in adults is commonly supposed to arise from large book-knowledge. It is simply a natural appetite for that provision of ideas and images which should, at this season, be laid in for the exercise of the higher faculties which have yet to come into use.—As I have said, I know from experience the state of things which exists when a child cannot help reading to an amount which the parents think excessive, and yet are unwilling, for good reasons, to prohibit. One Sunday afternoon, when I was seven years old, I was prevented by illness from going to chapel;—a circumstance so rare that I felt very strange and listless. I did not go to the maid who was left in the house, but lounged about the drawing-room, where, among other books which the family had been reading, was one turned down upon its face. It was a dull-looking octavo volume, thick, and bound in calf, as untempting a book to the eyes of a child as could well be seen: but, because it happened to be open, I took it up. The paper was like skim milk,—thin and blue, and the printing very ordinary. Moreover, I saw the word Argument,—a very repulsive word to a child. But my eye caught the word "Satan;" and I instantly wanted to know how anybody could argue about Satan. I saw that he fell through chaos, found the place in the poetry;—and lived heart, mind, and soul in Milton from that day till I was fourteen. I remember nothing more of that Sunday, vivid as is my recollection of the moment of plunging into chaos: but I remember that from that time till a young friend gave me a pocket edition of Milton, the calf-bound volume was never to be found because I had got it somewhere; and that, for all those years, to me the universe moved to Milton's music. I wonder how much of it I knew by heart—enough to be always repeating some of it to myself, with every change of light and darkness, and sound and silence,—the moods of the day, and the seasons of the year. It was not my love of Milton which required the forbearance of my parents,—except for my hiding the book, and being often in an absent fit. It was because this luxury had made me ravenous for more. I had a book in my pocket,—a book under my pillow; and in my lap as I sat at meals: or rather, on this last occasion it was a newspaper. I used to purloin the daily London paper before dinner, and keep possession of it,—with a painful sense of the selfishness of the act; and with a daily pang of shame and self-reproach, I slipped away from the table when the dessert was set on, to read in another room. I devoured all Shakspere, sitting on a footstool, and reading by firelight, while the rest of the family were still at table. I was incessantly wondering that this was permitted; and intensely, though silently grateful I was for the impunity and the indulgence. It never extended to the omission of any of my proper business. I learned my lessons; but it was with the prospect of reading while I was brushing my hair at bedtime; and many a time have I stood reading, with the brush suspended, till I was far too cold to sleep. I made shirts with due diligence,—being fond of sewing; but it was with Goldsmith, or Thomson, or Milton open on my lap, under my work, or hidden by the table, that I might learn pages and cantos by heart. The event justified my parents in their indulgence. I read more and more slowly, fewer and fewer authors, and with ever-increasing seriousness and reflexion, till I became one of the slowest of readers, and a comparatively sparing one.—Of course, one example is not a rule for all; but the number of ravenous readers among children is so large, and among adults so small in comparison, that I am disposed to consider it a general fact that when the faculties, naturally developed, reach a certain point of forwardness, it is the time for laying in a store of facts and impressions from books which are needed for ulterior purposes.

The parents' main business during this process is to look to the quality of the books read:—I mean merely to see that the child has the freest access to those of the best quality. Nor do I mean only to such as the parent may think good for a child of such and such an age. The child's own mind is a truer judge in this case than the parents' suppositions. Let but noble books be on the shelf,—the classics of our language,—and the child will get nothing but good.

The last thing that parents need fear is that the young reader will be hurt by passages in really good authors which might raise a blush a few years later. Whatever children do not understand slips through the mind, and leaves no trace; and what they do understand of matters of passion is to them divested of its mischief. Purified editions of noble books are monuments of wasted labour: for it ought to be with adults as it is with children;—their purity should be an all-sufficient purifier.

The second stage in the Intellectual Education of the Household children, then seems to be that in which the young creatures, having learned to use their own limbs and senses, and acquired the command of speech, begin to use their powers for the acquisition of materials for future thought. They listen, they look about them, they inquire, they read; and, above all, they dream. Life is for them all pictures. Everything comes to them in pictures. In preparation for the more serious work to come, the parent has chiefly to watch and follow Nature;—to meet the requirements of the child's mind, put the material of knowledge in its way, and furnish it with the arts necessary for the due use of its knowledge and its nobler powers: —the arts of reading, ready writing, and the recording and working of numbers; and the knowledge of the grammar of some one language, at least. Besides this, these best days of his memory should be used for storing up word-knowledge, and technical rules, and, as a luxury after these dry efforts, as much poetry as the pupil is disposed to learn; which will be a good deal, if the selection is, in any degree, left to his own choice: and some portion of it may well be so.

Thus far, here is nothing that may not be supplied in the most homely Household in the land, where there is any value for the human intellect, and any intention to educate the children. It is difficult to say what more could be done in the school-room of a palace. The intellect of the high and low is of the same nature, and developes itself in the same modes. While its training depends on the love and good sense of parents, as in this stage, it depends simply on the quality of the parents whether the children of the palace or of the cottage are the better educated.

"No mystery is here; no special boon

For high and not for low; for proudly graced,

And not for meek of heart."

# CHAPTER XXI.

## INTELLECTUAL TRAINING.—THE REASONING FACULTIES.—FEMALE EDUCATION.

The time comes at last,—sooner with one child, later with another,—when the superior faculties begin to show their activity; when the young pupil attempts to reason, and should be helped to reason well. The preparation for this time ought to have gone on during all the preceding years, in the establishment of a perfect understanding between his parents' minds and his own. He ought to have received nothing but truth from them, in their intellectual, as in all their other intercourse. What I mean is this. From the time he could speak, the child has no doubt asked the Why of everything that interested him. Now, no one knows the ultimate Why of anything whatever; and it is right to say this to the inquirer,—telling him as much as he can understand of the How; and it is but little that the wisest of us know of the How. For instance, the little thing cries out "O! there is a robin!" "A robin! and what is it doing?" "It is hopping about. It has picked up something. O! it is a worm. What does it get the worm for?" "To eat it. Robins eat a great many worms." "Why do they eat worms? Why does this robin eat that worm?" "Because it is hungry." No intelligent child will stop here. He will want to know why the robin does not eat anything rather than worms; why the robin is hungry; and certainly he will sooner or later wonder why there are robins at all. About these latter mysteries, the parent knows no more than the questioner: and he should say so. He may tell something of the how;—how the robin and all other living creatures are impelled to eat; how food gives nourishment; and so on. He may or may not, according to his judgment, give information, as far as he has it himself: but it ought not to be a matter of choice with him whether to put off a child with an unsatisfactory answer, or to declare truthfully his own ignorance. He must never weary of replying "I don't know," if fairly brought to this point, after telling what he does know. If he tells all that is understood of a tree and its growth, so that he thinks his child cannot possibly have more to ask, he will find there are other questions still to come. "Why are trees green?" If they are not all green, "Why is the red beech red, and the pine black?" "Why does a tree grow, instead of being always tall?" "Why is John Smith handsome while Tom Brown is ugly?" "Why do people exist when they could not tell beforehand whether they should like it or not?" Now, it will not do, if the child's mind is to be fairly dealt with, to give a dogmatical answer; to put off the inquirer with a form of words, or any assurance of anything that is not absolutely known to be true. "I do not know," is the answer which parental fidelity requires. "Does anybody know?" is the next question. "Nobody." "Shall I ever know?" "I don't think you will: but you can try when you grow up, if you like." Of course, the child determines to try when he is a man: and meantime, he is satisfied for the present. There is an understanding between his parent and himself, which will be of infinite use to him when his time comes for finding out truth for himself by a comparison of abstractions;— that is, by reasoning.

With some abstractions every child becomes early familiar; as the days of the week. Perhaps the first which he is able to use for purposes of reasoning are numbers. They are at least eminently useful as a link between tangible objects and those which are ideal. A child sees on the table that two pins added to two make four pins: and then that a button and a thimble put down beside a marble and a halfpenny make four things, as well as if they were all of the same sort. He thus receives into his mind the abstract notion of numbers. Whenever by his own thought, or by inquiry of others, he clearly sees that, because two sixes make twelve, four threes must make twelve, he has begun to reason. He has found out a truth by comparing an abstraction with an abstraction: that is, he has begun to reason. Having begun,—having once satisfaction in grasping an invisible truth in this way,—he will be disposed to go on: and I, for one, would allow him to do so, at his own pace. Nothing can be more foolish than to stimulate the reasoning faculties too early: but I do not see why their natural action should be repressed because of a theory that the reasoning faculties should not come into activity till such or such an age. I know how painful such repression is to a thoughtful child, and how useless is the attempt to stop the process, which will only be carried on with less advantage, instead of being put an end to. I knew a girl of eleven, thoughtful and timid, seldom venturing to ask questions, or to open her mind about what occupied it most,—who, on some unusual incitement to confidence during a summer evening walk, opened a theme of perplexity, to get a solution from a grown-up brother, whom she regarded as able to solve anything. She told him that she could not see how, if God foreknew everything, and could ordain everything, men could ever be said to sin against him, or be justly punished for anything they did: and then she went on to the other particular of that problem;—how, if God was all powerful to create happiness, and all good to desire it, there came to be any suffering in the world. Her brother answered her with kindness in his tone, but injudiciously. He told her that that was a very serious question which she was too young to consider yet; and that some years hence would be time enough. She was dissatisfied and hurt;— not from pride; but because she felt it hard to be left in a perplexity from which she fully supposed her brother could relieve her. She felt that if she could ask the question,—thus put in a definite form,—she must be capable of understanding the answer. And so she undoubtedly was. If the brother held the doctrine of free will, he should have replied that he did not know;— that he could not understand the perplexity any more than herself. If he held the necessarian doctrine, he should have imparted it to her; for her question showed that she was capable of receiving it. The end of the matter was that she suffered for years under that reply, never again venturing to propose her difficulty to any one. She worked her way through the soluble half of the question alone at last,—thinking first, and then reading, and then meditating again, till all was clear and settled; and in her mature years she found herself fast anchored on the necessarian doctrine,—rather wondering how she could have been so long in satisfying herself about a matter so clear, but aware that she had found an inestimable gain;—which she might have reposed upon some years earlier, if the natural working of her faculties had been trusted as it might have been.

Our enjoyment of our faculties appears to me to be more proportioned to their quality than their strength:—that, whether any one of us has the reasoning power, or the imagination stronger or weaker than the perceptive and conceptive faculties, he enjoys most the exercise of the higher. Certainly, children whose faculties are developed freely and fairly have an intense relish for reasoning, while the mind remains unwearied. The commonest topics voluntarily chosen are conduct and character; because the most familiar and interesting abstractions are those which are connected with morals. How boys and girls will debate by the hour together about the stoicism of Junius Brutus, and the patriotism of Brutus and Cassius; and about all the suicides of all Romans, and all the questionable acts of all heroes! The mother is the great resource here, because she is always at hand; and these matters are of such pressing importance to the little people, that they cannot wait till their father comes in, or can give them some of his evening leisure. These topics are good as an exercise of both the moral and intellectual powers: but they do not yield full satisfaction to the reasoning faculty, because they can never be brought to any certain and evident issue. The conclusions of morals are clear enough for practical guidance; but they are not proveable. For the full satisfaction of the reasoning faculties, therefore, children must set to work elsewhere. —They may get something of it out of their lessons in grammar, if they are trusted with the sense of the grammar they are taught: lighting upon an accusative case and a verb in a Latin sentence, they know there must be a nominative: and there it is presently, accordingly. Finding an ablative absolute, they are confident of finding some sort of proposition: and there it is, to their hand. The words on the page before them are as real to the sense as the written numerals on their slates: but behind both there is a working of unseen laws,—independent of the signification of either words or numerals,—whose operation and issue it is a deep-felt pleasure to follow and apprehend. The rules of grammar, and the laws of numbers,—(the rules of arithmetic, in short,)—are abstractions proceeding from abstractions; and their workings bring out a conclusion clear to the pupil's apprehension, and unquestionable. This is all exercise of the reasoning powers; and it is this exercise of those powers, or the use of ear and memory only which makes the difference between a pupil who learns grammar and arithmetic with the understanding or by rote.

I once witnessed a curious instance of the difference between the reasoning pupils of a class at school and the learners by rote. The test was, I think, designed by the master to be a test; and it answered his purpose even better than our strenuous exercises in grammar and arithmetic. Our master proposed to give some of us an idea of English composition, and said he would next week explain to us how to set about it. Some of us, however, were all on fire with the idea of writing essays, and were by no means disposed to wait. The next time our master entered the school-room, eight or ten pairs of beseeching eyes were fixed upon him; and he, being a good-natured man, asked what we wished. What we wanted was to be allowed immediately to write an essay on Music. He had no objection; but he asked for some precision in the object of the essay;—proposed that it should be the Uses of Psalmody, or some such topic, which could be treated in the limits of a school theme;—but no; he saw by the faces and manner of the class that it must be an essay on Music. I was the youngest of the class, who ranged from eleven to sixteen: and I wondered whether the elder ones felt as I did when I saw the little smile at the corners of the mouth, amidst the careful respect of our kind master. I felt that we were somehow doing something very silly, though I could not clearly see what. It was plain enough when we brought up our themes. Our master's respect and kindness never failed: and he now was careful to say that there was much that was true in each essay; but——. We saw the "but" for ourselves, and were ready to sink with shame; for nobody had courage to begin to laugh at our folly. Such a mass of rhapsody and rhodomontade as we presented to our master! Such highflying, incoherent nonsense! Each was pretty well satisfied with her own rhapsody till she heard the seven or nine others read. "Now, perhaps you perceive," our master began: and indeed we saw it all;—the lack of order and object;—the flimsiness,—and our own presumption. We were now more ready to be taught. Some, however, could not yet learn; and others liked this lesson better than any they had ever attempted. This is the difference which induces me to tell the story here. We were taught the parts of a theme, as our master and many others approved and practised them, in sermons and essays: and the nature and connexion of these parts were so clearly pointed out, that on the instant it appeared to me that a sudden light was cast at once on the processes of thought and of composition,—for both of which I had before an indistinct and somewhat oppressive reverence. I saw how the Proposition, the Reason, the Example, the Confirmation, and the Conclusion led out the subject into order and clearness, and, in fact, regularly emptied our minds of what we had to say upon it. From that day till our school was broken up (and my heart nearly broken with it) a year and a half afterwards, the joy of my life was writing themes;—or rather composing them; for the act of writing was terribly irksome. But that which some of us eminently enjoyed was altogether burdensome to others, from the procedure of the task being utterly unintelligible. I suppose their reasoning faculties were yet unawakened,—though they were not so very young. The Proposition they usually wrote down in the words in which our subject was given to us;—the mere title of the theme. The Reason was any sort of reason about any affair whatever,—the authors protesting that a reason was a reason any day. The Examples were begged, or copied out of any history book. The Confirmation was omitted, or declared to consist in "the universal experience of mankind,"—whatever the subject might be: and as for the Conclusion, that was easy enough:—it was only to say that for all the reasons given, the author concluded so and so,—in the words of the title. This was a case in which it would have been better to wait awhile, till the meaning of the task and its method should dawn upon the minds yet unready. But, for those who were capable, it was a task of great pleasure and privilege; and we loved our master for testing and trusting our faculties in a direction so new to us.

Those studies which require reasoning as a means to a proveable issue are of a high order, as regards both profit and pleasure: and boys and girls will be the better through life for whatever mathematical training their parents can procure for them. Be it little or be it much, they will have reason to be grateful as long as they live for what they can obtain. I mention girls, as well as boys, confident that every person able to see the right, and courageous enough to utter it, will sanction what I say. I must declare that on no subject is more nonsense talked, (as it seems to me) than on that of female education, when restriction is advocated. In works otherwise really good, we find it taken for granted that girls are not to learn the dead languages and mathematics, because they are not to exercise professions where these attainments are wanted; and a little further on we find it said that the chief reason for boys and young men studying these things is to improve the quality of their minds. I suppose none of us will doubt that everything possible should be done to improve the quality of the mind of every human being.—If it is said that the female brain is incapable of studies of an abstract nature,—that is not true: for there are many instances of women who have been good mathematicians, and good classical scholars. The plea is indeed nonsense on the face of it; for the brain which will learn French will learn Greek; the brain which enjoys arithmetic is capable of mathematics.—If it is said that women are light-minded and superficial, the obvious answer is that their minds should be the more carefully sobered by grave studies, and the acquisition of exact knowledge.— If it is said that their vocation in life does not require these kinds of knowledge,—that is giving up the main plea for the pursuit of them by boys;—that it improves the quality of their minds.—If it is said that such studies unfit women for their proper occupations,—that again is untrue. Men do not attend the less to their professional business, their counting-house or their shop, for having their minds enlarged and enriched, and their faculties strengthened by sound and various knowledge; nor do women on that account neglect the work-basket, the market, the dairy and the kitchen. If it be true that women are made for these domestic occupations, then of course they will be fond of them. They will be so fond of what comes most naturally to them that no book-study (if really not congenial to their minds) will draw them off from their homely duties. For my part, I have no hesitation whatever in saying that the most ignorant women I have known have been the worst housekeepers; and that the most learned women I have known have been among the best,—wherever they have been early taught and trained to household business, as every woman ought to be. A woman of superior mind knows better than an ignorant one what to require of her servants, how to deal with trades-people, and how to economise time: she is more clear-sighted about the best ways of doing things; has a richer mind with which to animate all about her, and to solace her own spirit in the midst of her labours. If nobody doubts the difference in pleasantness of having to do with a silly and narrow-minded woman and with one who is intelligent and enlightened, it must be clear that the more intelligence and enlightenment there is, the better. One of the best housekeepers I know,—a simple-minded, affectionate-hearted woman, whose table is always fit for a prince to sit down to, whose house is always neat and elegant, and whose small income yields the greatest amount of comfort, is one of the most learned women ever heard of. When she was a little girl, she was sitting sewing in the window-seat while her brother was receiving his first lesson in mathematics from his tutor. She listened, and was delighted with what she heard; and when both left the room, she seized upon the Euclid that lay on the table, ran up to her room, went over the lesson, and laid the volume where it was before. Every day after this, she sat stitching away and listening, in like manner, and going over the lesson afterwards, till one day she let out the secret. Her brother could not answer a question which was put to him two or three times; and, without thinking of anything else, she popped out the answer. The tutor was surprised, and after she had told the simple truth, she was permitted to make what she could of Euclid. Some time after, she spoke confidentially to a friend of the family,—a scientific professor,—asking him, with much hesitation and many blushes, whether he thought it was wrong for a woman to learn Latin. "Certainly not," he said;

"provided she does not neglect any duty for it.—But why do you want to learn Latin?" She wanted to study Newton's Principia: and the professor thought this a very good reason. Before she was grown into a woman, she had mastered the Principia of Newton. And now, the great globe on which we live is to her a book in which she reads the choice secrets of nature; and to her the last known wonders of the sky are disclosed: and if there is a home more graced with accomplishments, and more filled with comforts, I do not know such an one. Will anybody say that this woman would have been in any way better without her learning?—while we may confidently say that she would have been much less happy.

As for women not wanting learning, or superior intellectual training, that is more than any one should undertake to say in our day. In former times, it was understood that every woman, (except domestic servants) was maintained by her father, brother or husband; but it is not so now. The footing of women is changed, and it will change more. Formerly, every woman was destined to be married; and it was almost a matter of course that she would be: so that the only occupation thought of for a woman was keeping her husband's house, and being a wife and mother. It is not so now. From a variety of causes, there is less and less marriage among the middle classes of our country; and much of the marriage that there is does not take place till middle life. A multitude of women have to maintain themselves who would never have dreamed of such a thing a hundred years ago. This is not the place for a discussion whether this is a good thing for women or a bad one; or for a lamentation that the occupations by which women might maintain themselves are so few; and of those few, so many engrossed by men. This is not the place for a speculation as to whether women are to grow into a condition of self-maintenance, and their dependence for support upon father, brother and husband to become only occasional. With these considerations, interesting as they are, we have no business at this moment. What we have to think of is the necessity,—in all justice, in all honour, in all humanity, in all prudence,—that every girl's faculties should be made the most of, as carefully as boys'. While so many women are no longer sheltered, and protected, and supported, in safety from the world (as people used to say) every woman ought to be fitted to take care of herself. Every woman ought to have that justice done to her faculties that she may possess herself in all the strength and clearness of an exercised and enlightened mind, and may have at command, for her subsistence, as much intellectual power and as many resources as education can furnish her with. Let us hear nothing of her being shut out, because she is a woman, from any study that she is capable of pursuing: and if one kind of cultivation is more carefully attended to than another, let it be the discipline and exercise of the reasoning faculties. From the simplest rules of arithmetic let her go on, as her brother does, as far into the depths of science, and up to the heights of philosophy as her powers and opportunities permit; and it will certainly be found that the more she becomes a reasoning creature, the more reasonable, disciplined and docile she will be: the more she knows of the value of knowledge and of all other things, the more diligent she will be;—the more sensible of duty,—the more interested in occupations,—the more womanly. This is only coming round to the points we started from; that every human being is to be made as perfect as possible: and that this must be done through the most complete development of all the faculties.

# CHAPTER XXII.

## INTELLECTUAL TRAINING.—THE IMAGINATIVE FACULTIES.

The young mind is very well entertained for a time by the exercise of its reasoning powers,—if, instead of being baffled, they are encouraged and trained. But, there is a higher set of faculties still which begin to work ere long; and usually in such proportion to the reasoning powers as would seem to indicate some connexion between them. Or it may be that the moral fervour which gives great advantage to the reasoning powers is exactly that which is essential to the development of the highest of human faculties,—the Imagination. Certain it is that the children who most patiently and earnestly search out the reasons of things,—either looking deep into causes, or following them high up to consequences, are those who most strongly manifest the first stirrings of the heavenly power which raises them highest in the ranks of being known to exist. They may, or they may not, have shown a power of Fancy before this time. They may, or they may not, have manifested a strong conceptive faculty; a power of forming images of objects already well known or clearly described; but, if they can so think of unseen things, so compare them and connect them, as to bring truth out at last,—if, in short, they reflect and reason well, the probability is that they will prove to have a good portion of the higher faculty of Imagination. At least, we may be sure that a child of high imaginative faculty has good reasoning powers.

During the first exercise of the reasoning powers a child may, and probably will, become thoughtful. He will look grave at times, and be buried in reflection for awhile: but this gravity does not make him less cheerful; and when he has done thinking about the particular thing his head was full of, he is as merry as ever. But a little later, and his thoughtfulness becomes something quite different from this. If there is some mingling of melancholy with it, the parents must not be uneasy. It is all natural, and therefore right. He is beginning to see and to feel his position in the universe; to see and to feel that by the powers within him he is connected with all that exists, and can conceive of all that may exist: and his new consciousness gives a light to his eye and a meaning to his countenance that were never seen there before. While he was an infant, he was much like any other young animal for his thoughtless and unconscious enjoyment of all the good things that were strewed in his daily path. Then, he began to see deeper,—into the reasons of things, and their connexions; and now he had become higher than other young animals,—for they cannot perceive the truths of numbers, or discover by thought anything not before known in any science. But now, he has become conscious of himself; he can contemplate himself as he can contemplate any other object of thought; and he is occupied in connecting his own thoughts,—his own mind—with every object of thought. It is upon his consciousness and his thoughts united that his imaginative power has to act. By it, he sees everything in a new light, and feels everything with a new depth: and though he often finds this a glorious pleasure, he is sometimes much oppressed by it: and then comes the kind of gentle melancholy before referred to.

See the difference, to the child of dull imagination, or of an age too young for it, and the child superior in years or in faculty,—when they contemplate Nature, or Human Life, or anything whatever;—when they read the History of England, or Conversations on Chemistry, or Shakspere's Plays, or anything you please. Show them the sky as you are coming home at night. The one will learn to know the constellations as easily perhaps as the other, and will show somebody else the next night which is the Great Bear, and which is Orion: but the duller or younger child sees nothing more than what is before its eyes; or, if told that all those stars are worlds, believes it without seeing or feeling any thing beyond the mere fact as conveyed in the words. But at the same moment the faculty of Imagination in the other child is kindling up within him,—and kindling all his other powers. He sees, by his mind, far far beyond the bounds of human measurement and the human sight;—sees the universe full of rolling suns; worlds for ever moving in their circles, and never clashing; worlds of which there are myriads vaster than our own globe. All this he sees, not by gazing at the sky; for he sees it better when his head is on his pillow,—or when his hands are busy with some mechanical employment, the next day. If he feels how, with all his busy mind and swelling heart, and whole world of ideas, he is yet but an atom in this great universe, almost too small for notice, is not this enough to make him thoughtful? and if there is a tinge of melancholy in his seriousness, may it not be allowed for? Again, in reading the History of England,—the duller or younger child may remember the kings, and the great men, and the great battles, and the great famine and plague; and perhaps almost all the events told: and, if he has some considerable conceptive faculty, he may have pictures in his mind of the ancient Britons, and then of King Alfred and his people; and then of the Normans coming over and landing, and establishing themselves in our island. But the superior child sees all this, and very much more. The minds of all the people he reads of are as manifest to him as the events of their lives. He feels the wild valour of the old Britons while he reads of them; and his soul melts in reverence, and grief, and pity for King Alfred; and then it glows with courage; and then it grows calm with faith as he sees the courage and faith that were in King Alfred. And so on, through the whole history. And even more than this. He sees more than the individuals of whom he reads could see of themselves. The kingdom and the nation are ideas in his mind, as vivid as his idea of the personages he reads of. He feels when the nation is rising or falling; rejoices when a great and good man,—a sage, or a patriot, or a martyr—arises to bless his race, and burns with indignation and grief when the wicked have their own way. Is there not something here to make him thoughtful? and if there is a tinge of melancholy in his seriousness, may it not be allowed for? Suppose these two to read "Conversations on Chemistry," or "Scientific Dialogues,"—they will see and feel as differently as in the former cases. The inferior child will find some entertainment, and particularly if allowed to try chemical experiments: but these experiments will be to him a sort of cookery;—a putting things together, in order to succeed in producing some result,—amusing or pretty. His smattering of Chemistry is to him now a plaything, whatever it may become when he is wiser. But how different is it with the elder one, whose awakened imagination now silently enters with him into every chamber of his own mind and every scene of nature—opening his vision with a divine touch, and showing him everything in its vastness and its inner truth! He does not want to try chemical experiments. He would rather think quietly of the great agents of Nature, and see them, with the eye of his mind, for ever at their work;—Heat, spreading through all things, and even hiding in the polar ice;—Electricity, darting and streaming through all substances, and being the life of all that lives; and the flowing together and mixing of three airs to make air that we can breathe,—this flowing together and mixing having gone on ever since there were breathing creatures on the globe;—these great images, and those of the forces of the waters, the pressure of the atmosphere, the velocities of motion,—the mechanical action, in short, of the great forces of Nature, occupy and move him more than any outward methods of proof of what has been laid open to him. Or, if he tries experiments, the thing that impresses him is something far higher than amusement:—it is wonder and awe, and perhaps delight that he can put his hand in among the forces of Nature, and take his share, and set Nature to work for him. Is it any wonder that his heart throbs, and his eyes swim or kindle, and that he had rather think than speak? And may he not be left undisturbed at such a moment, till his mind takes a lower tone?

It is this faculty which has produced the highest benefits to the human race that it has ever enjoyed. The highest order of men who have lived are those in whom the power of Imagination has been the strongest, the most disciplined, and the most elevated. The noblest gifts that have been given to men are the ideas which have proceeded from such minds. It is this order of mind alone that creates. Others may discover, and adapt, and improve, and establish: but it is the imaginative order of mankind that creates,—whether it be the majestic steam-engine, or the immortal picture, or the divine poem. It should be a joyful thing to parents,—though it must be a very serious one,—to see clear tokens in any child of the development of this faculty,—the faculty of seeing things invisible,—of "seeing things that are not as though they were." If it is only of average strength, it is a true blessing, inasmuch as it ennobles the views and the life of the individual, if its benefit extends no further in a direct manner. If it appears in any marked degree, the parents' hearts cannot but be elated, though they may be anxious. It is a sign of natural nobility,—of a privilege higher than hereditary or acquired honour: and greater than a monarch can bestow. Through it, if it be rightly trained, its possessor must enjoy the blessings of largeness of heart and wealth of mind, and probably of being a benefactor, more or less, to his race.

Now,—what are the tokens of this endowment? and how should it be treated?

When a young person's views extend beyond the objects immediately presented to him, it is naturally seen in his countenance, manner, speech and habits. The questions he asks, the books he reads, his remarks on what he reads or hears, all show whether his mind is deeply employed. He is probably a great reader; and if he has been religiously brought up, he probably becomes intensely religious about the time of the development of his higher faculties.—He must be treated with great consideration and tenderness. If he is of an open disposition, apt to tell of his day dreams and aspirations, there must be no ridicule,—no disrespect from any part of the household. There ought to be none; for it is pretty certain that any day dreams and aspirations of his are more worthy of respect than any ridicule with which they can be visited. The way to strengthen and discipline his mind is not, as we have often said already, to repress any of its faculties, but to employ them well. In no case is this management more important than in the present.

Now, in this important period of youthful life, it is the greatest possible blessing if the son or daughter be on terms of perfect confidence with the mother. It is a kind of new life to a mother who has kept her mind and heart active and warm amidst her trials and cares, to enter into sympathy with the aspirations and imaginations of her ripening children. She has a keen enjoyment in the revival of her own young feelings and ideas;—some of the noblest she has known: and things which might appear extravagant at another time or from other persons, will be noble and animating as coming from those whose minds,—minds which she has watched from their first movements,—are now rapidly opening into comparative maturity. To her, then, the son or daughter need not fear to speak freely and openly. To her they may pour out their admiration of Nature, their wonder at the sublimities of science; their speculations upon character; their soundings in the abysses of life and death; their glorious dreams of what they will be and do. The more she sympathises with them in their intellectual pleasures and tendencies, the more will her example tell upon them as a conscientious doer of the small duties of life: and thus she may silently and unconsciously obviate one of the chief dangers of this period of her children's lives. If they see that the mother who glows with the warmth of their emotions, and goes abroad through the universe hand in hand, as we may say, with them, to note and enjoy all that is mighty and beautiful, all that is heroic and sweet,—is yet as punctual in her every day duty as the merest plodder and worldling, they will take shame to themselves for any reluctance that they feel to commonplace ideas and what seems to them drudgery. Full confidence and sympathy are the first requisites of the treatment of this period.

But the wise parent will have laid up material for the employment of the imaginative faculty, long before it can appear in any strength. The child will have been familiarised with a high and noble order of ideas; and especially of moral ideas: for the picturesque or scientific will be pretty sure to make themselves duly appreciated by the awakened ideal faculties. Whatever the parent can tell of heroic conduct, of lofty character, of the grave crises and affecting changes of human life, will be so much material laid in for the virtuous and salutary use of those awakening faculties which might otherwise be occupied in selfishness and other mischief. Let the mind be abundantly ministered to. This may be done in the most homely households where there is any nobility of mind. Every parent has known some person who is noble and worthy of contemplation for character and conduct. Every parent can tell some moving or striking tale of a human lot. To all, the heavens and the earth, the sea, and all that in them is, are open for contemplation. In every household, there is the Bible: and in the houses of all who read this, there is, no doubt, Milton, on the shelf beside the Bible. With these parents have means enough for the education of their children's highest faculties. In these they hold a greater treasure than any other that can be found in royal abodes: and the kingdom of Nature is a field which their children have free license to rove with the highest. Let them have and enjoy these treasures abundantly. Let them read all tales of noble adventure that can be obtained for them;—of the heroes that have struggled through Polar ice and burning African sands; that have sailed on past the horizon of hope in the discovery of new continents, and have succeeded through faith, courage and patience. Let the reading of good fiction be permitted, where the desire is strong. Some of the highest interests of English history have been opened to the present generation by the novels of Scott, as to many a preceding one by the Plays of Shakspere. My own opinion is that no harm is done, but much good, by an early reading of fiction of a high order: and no one can question its being better than leaving the craving mind to feed upon itself,—its own dreams of vanity or other selfishness,—or to seek an insufficient nourishment from books of a lower order. The imagination, once awakened, must and will work, and ought to work. Let its working be ennobled, and not debased, by the material afforded to it.

In the parents' sympathy must be included forbearance; forbearance with the uncertainty of temper and spirits, the extravagance of ideas, the absurd ambition, or fanaticism or, (as it is generally called) "romance" which show themselves more or less, on the opening of a strong imaginative faculty. It should be remembered that the young creature is half-living in a new world; and that the difficulty of reconciling this beloved new world with the familiar old one is naturally very trying to one who is just entering upon the struggles of the mind and of life. He cannot reconcile the world and its ways and its people with the ideals which are presenting themselves to him; and he becomes, for a time, irritable, or scornful, or depressed. One will be fanatical, for a time, and sleep on the boards, and make and keep a vow never to smile. Another will be discontented, and apparently ungrateful, for a time, in the idea that he might be a hero if he had certain advantages which are not given him. Another looks down already on all his neighbours on account of the great deeds he is to do by and by: and all are convinced,—every youth and maiden of them all,—that nobody can enter into their feelings,—nobody understand their minds,—nobody conceive of emotions and aspirations like theirs. At the moment, this is likely to be true; for their ideas and emotions are vast and stirring, beyond their own power to express; and it can scarcely happen that any one is at hand, just at the right season, to receive their out-pourings, and give them credit for more than they can tell.—With all the consequences of these new movements of the mind, the parents must have forbearance,—even to the point (if it must be) of witnessing an intimacy with some young companion, not very wise, who is the depository of more confidence than is offered to those who should be nearest and dearest. These waywardnesses and follies may have their day, and prove after all to have been, in their way, wholesome discipline. Every waywardness brings its smart; and every folly leaves its sting of shame in the mind that is high enough to manifest any considerable power of imagination. They will punish and cure themselves; and probably in a short time. Nature may be trusted here, as everywhere. If we have patience to let her work, without hindrance and without degradation, she will justify our confidence at last. Give her free scope,—remove out of her way everything that is low and sordid, and needlessly irritating, and minister to her everything that is pure and gentle, and noble and true, and she will produce a glorious work. In the wildest flights of haughty and undisciplined imagination, the young aspirant will take heed enough to the beauty and dignity of a lowly, and dutiful and benignant walk in life, to come down and worship it when cruder visions have passed away. It is only to wait, in gentleness and cheerfulness, and the wild rhapsodist, or insolent fanatic will work his way through his snares into a new world of filial, as well as other duty, and, without being less of a poet, but because he is more of one, will be a better son and brother and neighbour,—making his life his highest poem.

It will be said that we have here, in treating of the training of the Intellectual faculties, recurred to the department of morals. And this is true. No part of human nature can work in isolation; and when we treat of any function by itself, it is for the convenience of our understandings, and not as a following of nature. No intellectual faculty can act independently of the moral; and the higher the faculties, the closer we find their interaction; till we arrive at the fact that Veneration, Benevolence, Hope, Conscientiousness and Firmness cannot act to perfection except in company with a vigorous faculty of Imagination, and strong Reflective powers: and again, that the Reasoning and Imaginative powers can never work to their fullest capacity unless the highest of the moral powers are as active as themselves. In all true poetry, there is a tacit appeal to the sanction of Conscience, and Veneration and Benevolence are the heavenly lights which rise upon the scene: while, on the other hand, no Reverence is so deep, Benevolence so pure, as those which are enriched by the profoundest Thought, and refined and exalted by the noblest Idealism.

These truths bring us to a practical consideration as serious as any which our minds can receive and dwell upon. My own sense of it is so strong, and so confirmed by the experience of a life, that I feel that if I had the utmost power of thought and language that were ever possessed by the human being, I could do no justice to it:—that the only means of improving the morale to the utmost is by elevating the ideal of the individual. It is well to improve the conduct, and satisfy the conscience of the child by calling upon its resolution to amend its faults in detail,—to control its evil tempers, and overcome its indolence and laxity: but this is a temporary method, insufficient for its ultimate needs. The strength of resolution fails when the season of youth is past, or is employed on other objects; and it is rare, as we all know, to see faults amended, and bad habits overcome in mature years: and then, if improvement proceeds, radically and continuously, it is by the mind being placed under good influences, operating both powerfully and continuously. Of good influences, the most powerful and continuous is the presence in the mind of a lofty ideal. This is the great central fire which is always fed by the material it draws to itself, and which can hardly be extinguished. When the whole mind is possessed with the image of the godlike, ever growing with the expansion of the intelligence, and ever kindling with the glow of the affections, every passion is consumed, every weakness grows into the opposite strength; and the entire force of the moral life, set free from the exclusive care of the details of conduct, and from the incessant anxiety of self-regards, is at liberty to actuate the whole harmonious being in its now necessary pursuit of the highest moral beauty it can conceive of. To this godlike inspiration, strong and lofty powers of Thought and Imagination are essential: and if parents desire that their children should be what they are made to be,—"but a little lower than the angels,"—they must cherish these powers as the highest sources of moral inspiration.

# CHAPTER XXIII.
## CARE OF THE HABITS.—IMPORTANCE OF HABIT.

The importance of Habit is an old subject; as old as any in morals. For thousands of years, moralists and philosophers have written and preached about it; and everybody is convinced by what they say. But I much doubt whether, even yet, many penetrate into the depth of the matter. Everybody sees, and everybody has felt the difficulty of breaking bad habits, and that there is no security to virtue so strong as long-formed good habits: but my observation compels me to think that scarcely anybody is aware of the whole truth;—that every human being (except such as are born defective) might be made perfectly good if his parents were wise enough to do all that might be done by the power of Habit. This seems a bold thing to say, but I am convinced that it is true.

I am aware that we cannot expect to see any parents wise enough to know how to make the fullest use of this power: and perhaps there are none, even of the tenderest parents, who can keep themselves up to an incessant vigilance over their infants, without any carelessness or flagging. Sometimes they are busy; sometimes they are tired; sometimes they are disheartened. They are not perfectly wise and good themselves; and therefore they must sink below the mark, more or less. But I am sure it would be a great help to their strength, and vigilance, and heartiness, if they could clearly see how easily their children may be made anything they please.

The great points, for conscientious parents, are to be fully convinced of the supreme importance of the formation of Habits, and to begin early enough. If they will begin early enough, they will be sure to be convinced. But a pretty strong conviction may be had beforehand, by observation of the history and character of mankind.

Habits of Belief are the most important of all: and everybody thinks so: and of all Beliefs those which relate to Duty,—those which are called religious—are the highest. Now look round the world, and see how many individuals you can find who have inquired out for themselves what they think they believe. As for nations,—a nation of independent thinkers is a thing never dreamed of. Such a spectacle as that has never been seen in the wildest visions of the most sanguine of poets and moralists. I have travelled among heathens, Mohammedans, Jews, and many kinds of Christians; and I have found them all believing what they were taught, before they could reason, to hold as sacred truth; and this was exactly what their teachers were themselves taught to suppose (for one cannot call this Belief) in the same manner. The Red Indian, on the shores of the American lakes, and on the wide prairie, is brought up, from the time he can understand language at all, to believe that there is a Great Spirit who lives far away over the waters or beyond the forests, who is jealous and angry if the people do not offer to him whatever they like best;—who forbids them to touch whatever he wants for himself;—who has favourites among their warriors, and is most pleased with those who most torture their bodies, to show their bravery. The Indian believes in a good many inferior spirits, who do him good or harm, and mingle more in his affairs than the Great Spirit does. This is the Indian way of thinking; and every Indian child grows up to think in the same way, upon the whole, though one may be more sure than another of one or another part of the doctrine. No one of the whole tribe asks for any proof that things are so. The early habit of taking these doctrines for granted, as something solemn and sacred, which somebody must have known for true a long time ago, prevents any one but a thoughtful person here and there ever inquiring whether there is really any knowledge existing about the matter at all, or only superstition. Then, there are the Jews. Not one Jew in ten thousand ceases to be a Jew in religion; and nobody out of the Jewish body ever gets to think as they do;—to hold their doctrines, and their traditions, and their superstitions. Next, in order of time, come the Christians. There are many bodies of Christians, differing as much from one another as if they held faiths called by different names. There are the Christians of the Greek Church, worshipping many gods under the name of saints;—some thinking it blasphemy not to adore the Emperor of Russia next to God, and some paying their first homage to the Virgin with Three Hands. There are the Christians of the Romish Church, who are shocked at the Emperor of Russia for not being one of them; and shocked at the Protestants for not worshipping the bones and toe-nails of their saints. And there are the Protestant Christians, who are shocked at the superstitions of the Romish Church on the one hand, and at the doctrines of every Protestant sect but their own, on the other. Then come the Mohammedans, who think it exactly as impious in all Christians not to receive Mohammed, their prophet, whom they think a greater than Christ, as the Christians think it impious in the Jews not to receive Christ, whom they hold to be greater than Moses. The children of all these multitudes, (except in an extremely rare case, here and there) receive what they are early told, as their parents received it before them; and no one supposes that any one of those vast multitudes would think and feel as he does on matters of religion if he were not early habituated to think and feel as he does. Can we imagine any one of ourselves, concluding for ourselves, for instance, that the most solemn and sacred of human duties was to go through a set of prostrations and gestures, like those of the Mohammedans, five times a day as long as we live, unless we were taught, from early infancy, to consider such acts to be in the highest degree virtuous? Can we imagine ourselves thinking, as the Mohammedans do, that every man who does not go through this set of gestures five times every day, is careless about goodness altogether,—is an Infidel (which is the Mohammedan name for a Christian)—is wicked, and must be cast into hell? More persons in the world believe this than believe in the gods of the Red Indian, and the faith of the Jews, and the doctrines of all bodies of Christians put together. Yet it is incredible that any man would so believe,—so undoubtingly, so solemnly, if he had not been habituated to such a belief from the very beginning. If the beliefs of the majority of mankind are thus dependant upon habit,—if their faith and their views of duty and happiness,—(the most important of all views) have this origin, how is it possible to overrate the importance of Habit? If, turning away from the Greek Christians and the Mohammedans, we contemplate in our imagination a large sect or nation who should have been habituated, from the first dawning of intelligence, to regard perfect goodness as the most sacred and solemn and beautiful thing that the human mind can conceive of,—as a thing the most interesting and important to every human being,—and a thing within the reach of every one of us, is it conceivable that such a people would not be the most virtuous ever seen on earth? Let it not be said that children are so taught,—that such is the habit of their minds in our Christian country: for alas! it is very much otherwise. They are occasionally told, indeed, that Christ desired his followers to be perfect as their Father in heaven is perfect; but this is not the aim steadily and cheerfully set before any child, as a hopeful enterprise,—as the best thing in the world, and as a thing which must be done. No child sees that this object is what his parents are living for, in comparative disregard of everything else; and that this is what he ought to live for, and is expected certainly to accomplish, according to his means. While he is told, and pretty often, that the best thing in the world is to be good, he is habituated, by what he sees and hears almost all day long, to believe that it is a hopeless thing to become perfectly good, and that everybody tries, in fact, for something else, with more zeal and expectation;—to get knowledge, to get reputation, to get employment and comfort,—to get all manner of pleasant things by their own desires and exertions, while they trust that some power will make them good, without that unremitting desire and exertion on their parts which alone can make them so.

I have before me the Remarks of a conscientious and affectionate father on the essential and unlimited power of Habit in the rearing of Children;—a truth which he had heard of all his life, but never fairly estimated till he had employed his energies on the education of his own family. I do not know who he is; but I see by the pamphlet before meA that he is earnest and intelligent, and qualified to speak from experience. Earnest he must be, for it appears that it was his constant habit, during the infancy of his children, to rise in the night, to see that they were well, and sleeping peacefully: and he invariably went with them to school, and met them at the school door, to bring them home again,—more than a mile,—though he was a busy man,—obliged to work for their bread and his own. This earnest observer says "I now repeat the opinion that every child born, not insane or idiotic, might, to a moral certainty, be trained to be a gentle, a benevolent, and a pious adult. Of the correctness of this opinion I have long ceased to have any doubt. Holding this opinion to be positively correct, I next held that the universal belief of its correctness would soon lead to an amount of improvement in the several conditions of human existence that would exceed even my own sanguine expectations. The encouragement which this belief would give to parents would bring into active and affectionate exertion an amount of attention and devotion to the training of the infant feelings and propensities of their offspring, such as heretofore has never been exercised, or perhaps ever imagined. I would, therefore, spread this belief among all mankind, by every means in my power to employ, and with it my opinions of the kind of teaching, or rather training, by which such blessed results might be produced. To describe this kind of teaching, or training, is not at present in my power to do, to a due extent. I will but give one brief rule, namely, 'What you wish a child to be, be that to the child.' And I would impress upon the mind of the mother, the nurse, or other teacher, the importance of so training each desire or propensity as to bring it as early as possible into habitual obedience to the dictates of the religious and moral sentiments,—those sentiments being guided by the enlightened intellect of such mother, nurse, or teacher. These teachers should be aware of the fact that the mind of a child is continually acquiring habits of thought, as its limbs are habits of action, whether by the spontaneous and unguided efforts of its own mind and body, or by following the training of those having the care of it. They should be continually improving themselves in the art of so guiding the infant dispositions, and the exercises and actions of their charge as to form the disposition as early as possible; and this course of training would effectually preserve the child from every approach to the formation of any other habits than those inculcated by the teacher."—(Remarks, &c., pp. , ).

A "Remarks on the Advantages of early Training and Management of Children." By a Colonist. Ollivier, , Pall-Mall.

Next to the Beliefs established by early habit, come the propensities. Under this head, nothing more can be necessary than to relate an anecdote which teaches much more eloquently than any thing I can say out of my own convictions. In North America, a tribe of Indians attacked a white settlement, and murdered the few inhabitants. A woman of the tribe, however, carried away a very young infant, and reared it as her own. The child grew up with the Indian children, different in complexion, but like them in every thing else. To scalp the greatest possible number of enemies was, in his view, the most glorious and happy thing in the world. While he was still a youth, he was seen by some white traders, and by them conducted back to civilised life. He showed great relish of his new way of life, and, especially, a strong desire of knowledge, and a sense of reverence which took the direction of religion; so that he desired to become a clergyman. He went through his college course with credit, and was ordained. He fulfilled his function well, and appeared happy and satisfied. After a few years, he went to serve a settlement somewhere near the seat of war, which was then going on between Great Britain and the United States; and before long, there was fighting not far off. I am not sure whether he was aware that there were Indians in the field, (the British having some tribes of Indians for allies,) but he went forth to see how matters were going;—went forth in his usual dress,—black coat, and neat white shirt and neckcloth. When he returned, he was met by a gentleman of his acquaintance, who was immediately struck by an extraordinary change in the expression of his face;—by the fire in his eye, and the flush on his cheek;—and also by his unusually shy and hurried manner. After asking news of the battle, the gentleman observed, "but you are wounded.—Not wounded!—why, there is blood upon the bosom of your shirt." The young man crossed his hands firmly, though hurriedly upon his breast; and his friend, supposing that he wished to conceal a wound which ought to be looked to, pulled open his shirt and saw—what made the young man let his hands fall in despair. From between his shirt and his breast, the gentleman took out—a bloody scalp. "I could not help it," said this poor victim of early habit, in an agonised voice. He turned, and ran too swiftly to be overtaken; betook himself to the Indians, and never more appeared among the whites. No one supposes that there was any hypocrisy in this man while he was a clergyman. No one doubts that he would have lived a contented life of piety, benevolence and study, if he had never come within sight or sound of war. When he did so, up rose his early habitual combative and destructive propensities, overthrowing in an instant all later formed convictions and regenerated feelings. By the extent of victory here, we may form some idea of the force of early Habit, or be duly warned by the question whether we can form any idea of it.

The first habit to be formed is,—as is self-evident,—that of obedience; for this is a necessary preliminary to the formation of all other habits. If mothers would but believe it, there is nothing in the world easier than to form a habit of implicit obedience in any child. Every child,—dependant and imitative,—is obedient as a matter of course if nature is not early interfered with, and put out of her way. Every one must see that good sense on the part of the mother is absolutely necessary,—to observe what the course of nature is, and to adapt her management to it. For instance,—there is no way in which infants are more frequently, or so early, taught disobedience as by being teased for kisses. The mother does so love her infant's kiss,—to see the little face put up when the loving desire is spoken,—that she can never have enough of it. But her sense, and her sympathy with her little one show her that it is not the same thing with the child. Well as it loves caresses in due measure, it can easily be fretted by too many of them; and if the mother persists in requiring too many while the infant is eager after something else, she will first have to put up with a hasty and reluctant kiss, and will next have to witness the struggles of the child to avoid it altogether. If too young to slip from her arms, he will hide his face:—if he can walk, he will run away, and not come back when she calls. She has made him disobedient by asking of him more than he is yet able to give. If the training begins by pleasantly bidding him do what it is easy and pleasant to him to do, he will do it, as a matter of course. When it is to him a matter of course to do as he is bid, he will prove capable of doing some things that he does not like,—if desired in the usual cheerful and affectionate tone. He will go to his tub in the cold morning, and take physic, and be quiet when he wants to romp;—all great efforts to him. And he will get on, and become capable of greater and greater efforts, if his faculties of opposition and pride be not roused by any imprudence, and if his understanding be treated with due respect by the appeals to his obedience being such only as are moderate and reasonable.

He must be left as free as reason and convenience allow, that his will may not be too often crossed, and his temper needlessly fretted. What he is not to have, but would certainly wish for, must be put out of his sight, if possible. If there are any places where he must not go, he should see it to be impossible to get into them:—for instance, it is better that the fire should be well guarded than the child forbidden to go upon the rug;—and in either case, his gay playthings should not stand on the mantel-piece, tempting him to climb for them.—And so on,—through the round of his day. Let his little duties and obligations be made easy to him by sense and sympathy on the part of his parents; and then let them see that the duty is done,—the obligation fulfilled.

All this is easy enough; and certainly, from all that I have ever been able to observe, I am convinced that success,—perfect success in forming a habit of obedience is always possible. Where a whole household acts in the same good spirit towards the little creature who has to be trained,—where no one spoils him and no one teases him,—he will obey the bidding of the voice of gentle authority in all he does, as simply as he obeys the bidding of Nature when he eats and sleeps.

So much for this preliminary habit, which is essential to the formation of all others that the parents wish to guide and establish. I will now speak briefly of the Personal and Family Habits which are the manifestation of those conditions of mind of which I have treated in my preceding chapters.

# CHAPTER XXIV.
## CARE OF THE HABITS.—PERSONAL HABITS.

It requires some little consideration to feel sufficiently that it is as necessary to be explicit and earnest about the personal habits of children as about their principles, temper, and intellectual state. Our personal habits have become so completely a second nature to us, that it requires some effort to be aware how far otherwise it is with the young,—how they have every thing to learn; and what a serious thing it is to everybody at some time of his life to learn to wash his own face and button his own jacket. The conviction comes across one very powerfully in great houses, where little lords and ladies are seen to need teaching in the commonest particulars of manners and habits, as much as any young creatures about a cottage door. Every one knows this as a matter of fact; but still, there is something odd in seeing children in velvet tunics and lace frocks, and silk stockings and satin shoes, holding up their little noses,—or not holding them up—to the maternal pocket-handkerchief; or dropping fruit-stones and raisin-stalks into papa's coat-collar, by climbing up behind his chair. To see this natural rude ness in those to whom consummate elegance is hereafter to appear no less natural, makes one thoughtful for the sake of such as are to remain comparatively rude through life; and also because it reminds one that there is nothing in regard to all personal habits, that children have not to learn.

It is so very serious a matter to them,—the attainment of good personal habits,—that they ought to be aided to the utmost by parental consideration. This consideration is shown first in the actual help given to the child by its mother's hands; and afterwards by making all the arrangements of the household as favourable as possible to good habits in each individual.

The tender mother makes the times of washing and dressing gay and pleasant to her little infant by the play and caresses which she loves to lavish even more than the child delights to receive. She can hardly overvalue the influence of these seasons on the child's future personal habits. Hurry, rough handling, silence, or fretfulness may make the child hate the idea of washing and dressing, for long years afterwards; while the associations of a season of play and lovingness may help on the little creature a long way in the great work of taking care of its own person. When the time comes,—the proud time,—when it may stand by itself to wash, the pride and novelty help it on; and it is rather offended if help interferes, to prevent its being exposed too long to the cold. All this is very well; but there comes a time afterwards when the irksomeness of washing and dressing, and cleaning teeth, and brushing hair, becomes a positive affliction to some children, such as no parents that I have known seem to have any idea of. We grown people can scarcely remember the time when these operations were not to us so purely mechanical as that our minds are entertained by ideas all the time, as much as if we were about any other business. But children are not so dexterous, in the first place; in the next, all labour of which they know the extent is very oppressive to them: and again, any incessant repetition of what they in any degree dislike is really afflictive to them. We must remember these things, or we shall not understand the feebleness of will which makes a boy neglect some part of his morning washing, and a girl the due hair-brushing in the evening, though both are aware that they suffer more in conscience as it is, than they could from the trouble, if they could rouse themselves to do the business properly. I have known one child sick of life because she must, in any circumstances, clean her teeth every day;—every day for perhaps seventy years. I have known of a little boy in white frocks who sat mournfully alone, one autumn day, laying the gay fallen vine-leaves in a circle, and thinking how tired he was of life,—how dreadfully long it was, and full of care. Its machinery overpowered him. I knew a girl, old enough to be reproached for the badness of her handwriting,—(and she was injudiciously reproached, without being helped to mend it)—who suffered intensely from this, and even more from another grief;—she had hair which required a good deal of care, and she was too indolent to keep it properly. These were the two miseries of her life; and they did make her life miserable. She did not think she could mend her handwriting; but she knew that she might have beautiful hair by brushing it for ten minutes longer every night: yet she could not do it. At last, she prayed fervently for the removal of these two griefs,—though she knew the fable of the Waggoner and Hercules. Now,—in cases like these, help is wanted. Remonstrance, disgrace, will not do, in many cases where a little sympathy and management will. Cannot these times be made cheerful, and the habit of painful irresolution broken, by putting the sinner into the company of some older member of the family, or by employing the thoughts in some pleasant way while the mechanical process is going on?—I mean only while the difficulty lasts. When habits of personal cleanliness have become fixed and mechanical, it is most desirable (where it can by any means be managed) for each child to be alone,—not only for the sake of decency, but for the benefit of the solitude and silence, morning and night, which are morally advantageous for everybody old enough to meditate.

I fear it is still necessary to teach and preach that nobody has a right to health who does not wash all over every day. This is done with infants; and the practice should never be discontinued. Every child of a family should look upon this daily complete washing in cold water as a thing as completely of course as getting its breakfast. There was a time, within my remembrance, when even respectable people thought it enough to wash their feet once a week; and their whole bodies when they went to the coast for sea-bathing in August. In regard to popular knowledge of the Laws of Health, our world has got on: and, after the expositions, widely published, of those who enable us to understand the Laws of Health, we may hope that washing from head to foot is so regular an affair with all decent people as to leave no doubt or irresolution in children's minds about how much they shall wash, any day of the year.—As for the care of the teeth,—parents ought to know that, in the opinion of dentists, all decay of the teeth proceeds from the bone of which the teeth are composed not being kept purely clean and bright. This happens oftenest when teeth overlap, or grow so that every part cannot be reached. Much of this may be remedied, if not all of it, by early application to a dentist. But parents to whom this precaution is impossible can do much to save their children from future misery from toothache, and indigestion through loss of teeth, by seeing that the tooth-scrubbing is properly performed. This is more important than the polishing of knives and brass knockers.—As for the brushing of a girl's long hair, it really is a very irksome business till it becomes mechanical; and a mother may consider a little effort at amusement well bestowed till the habit of doing it properly is securely formed, and the mind is rich enough to entertain itself the while.

Readers begin to yawn or skip when they meet, in any book, with praises of early rising. Yet how can I pass over this particular of personal habits, when I think it of eminent importance?—I believe it is rare to see such early rising as I happen to think desirable. I believe it is rare to see families fairly at their daily work by eight o'clock,—after having had out-door exercise and breakfast; and this, every morning in the year. The variety of objects presented for the observation and enjoyment of children (and of everybody else) in the early morning hours, far surpasses that which can be seen at any other time of day. Even town-bred children can see more pure sky, and quieter streets, and the country seems to have come nearer. And in the country, there are more animals abroad,—more squirrels, more field mice, more birds, than at noon or in the evening. The rooks fly higher in the dawn than at any other time; the magpies are bolder and droller; the singing birds in the thickets beyond measure more gleeful; and one need not tell that this is the hour for the lark. All except very young children can keep themselves warm in the mid-winter mornings, and will enjoy the delight of being out under the stars, and watching the last fragment of the moon, hanging over the eastern horizon, clear and bright in the breaking dawn. When these children come in, warm, rosy, and hungry, at seven o'clock, or half-past, and sit down to their breakfast, they seem hardly of the same order of creatures with such as come sauntering down from their chambers, when their parents have half done their meal;—sauntering because they are tired with dressing, or have had bad dreams, and have not recovered their spirits. And what a difference it makes in the houses of rich and poor whether the breakfast things are standing about till nearly ten o'clock, or whether the family have by that time been at work for nearly two of the brightest, and freshest, and quietest, hours of the day!

In every industrious household there should be a bell. This is an admonition which tries no tempers, and gives no personal offence. If the father himself rings the family up in the mornings, it is a fine thing for everybody. If he cannot,—if he is too weary with his day's work for early rising, or if the mother is disturbed with her baby in the night,—if neither parent can be early in the morning, then let it not be insisted on that the children shall be so. It is a less evil that they should forego all the advantages of early rising than that any contest on the subject should take place between them and their parents. I have seen cases where the parents could not, or did not, appear till nine o'clock or later, but yet made it a point of conscience with the children to be early;—with the most disastrous effect. The children were conscientious, and they did try. When they now and then succeeded, they were satisfied and triumphant, and thought they should never fail again. But the indolence of the growing season of life was upon them: and there was the languor of waiting for breakfast. In the summer mornings, they were chilly and languid over their books; and in the winter, the fire made them sleepy. They grew later and later; they were rebuked, remonstrated with,—even warned against following the example of their parents: but they sank deeper into indolence. At last, the suffering of conscience became so great that it was thrown off by a most audacious effort. I happened to be a witness to the incident; and I have never lost the impression of it. The two girls were only half-dressed at half-past eight. They heard their mother's door open, and looked at each other. She came (herself only half-dressed) to say that she had been defied long enough, and she would be obeyed. She slapped them heartily. As she shut the door, the younger sister, all horror and dismay, stole a look at the elder. The elder laughed; and the younger was evidently delighted to join. I saw, on the instant, that it was all over with the mother's authority. The spirit of defiance had risen, and burst the bonds of conscience. Late rising,—the very latest,—curse as it is,—is better than this. What a struggle is saved in such cases—what a cost of energy, and health, and conscience, by a complete establishment of good habits, through the example of the parents! If the father be but happy enough to be able to take out his little troop into the fields, or merely for a stretch along the high road, in the freshness of the morning, what a gain there is on every hand! He has the best of their affections, if he can make himself their companion at this most cheery hour of the day; and they will owe to him a habit which not only enhances the enjoyment of life, but positively lengthens its duration. Then, after their walk of a mile or two, they find mother and breakfast awaiting them at home,—the house in order and already aired; and everything ready for business when the morning meal is done. They are in the heart of their work, whatever it be, when their neighbours are opening their chamber doors. In London, I am aware, one meets with the plea, in every case, that early rising is impossible, on account of the lateness of the hours of everybody else. I only know that when I lived in lodgings in London, I used to boil my coffee on the table at seven o'clock,—giving no trouble to servants,—and that I used to think it pleasant to have my pen in hand at half-past seven,—the windows open to the fresh watered streets, and shaded with summer blinds, and the flower-girls stationing themselves below,—their gay baskets of roses still wet with dew. I think London streets pleasanter in the dawn than at any other time. In country towns, I know that families can and do keep early hours, without any real difficulty: and in the country, everybody can do as he pleases. I need not say that growing children must have their breakfast before they feel any exhaustion for want of it. I do not understand the old-fashioned method of early rising;—working hard for three or four hours before eating anything at all. If adults can bear this, it is certain that children cannot. I may mention here that a prime means of health for persons of all ages is to drink abundance of cold water on rising, and during the vigorous exercise of the early morning. This morning regimen, if universally adopted, would save the doctors of our island half their work.

There is no part of the personal habits of children more important than that which relates to their eating. We must remember how vivid the pleasures of the senses are to children,—how strong their desire of every kind of gratification,—and how small their store, as yet, of those intellectual and moral resources which make grown people careless of the pleasures of sense. If we look back to our own childhood, and remember our intense pleasure in looking at brilliant colours, and at hearing sweet sounds, unconnected with words and ideas,—such as the chords of an Eolian harp,—and the thrill of pleasure we had at the sight of a favourite dish upon the table, we shall be aware that, however ridiculous such emotions appear to us now, they are realities which must be taken into account in dealing with children.—The object is so to feed children as to give them the greatest amount of relish which consists with their health of body and mind. If their appetites are not considered enough, they will suffer in body; if too much, they will suffer infinitely more in mind. I have seen both extremes; and I must say, I think the consequences so important as to deserve more consideration than the subject usually meets with.

In one large family which I had for some time the opportunity of observing, there was a pretty strict discipline kept up throughout, with excellent effect on the whole; but in some respects it was carried too far. Some of the children were delicate, particularly in stomach; and the intention of the parents was that this should be got over, as better for the children than yielding to it. Three or four of the children throve well on the basin of bread and milk, which was the breakfast of them all: but there was one little girl who never could digest milk well; and the suffering of that child was evident enough. She did not particularly dislike milk; and she never asked for any thing else. That would have been, in her eyes, a piece of shocking audacity. She had a great reverence for rules; and she seemed never to dream of any rule being set aside for her sake, however hardly it might bear upon her. So she went on for years having the feeling of a heavy lump in her throat for the whole of every morning,—sometimes choking with it, and sometimes stealing out into the yard to vomit; and, worse than the lump in the throat, she had depression of spirits for the first half of every day, which much injured the action of her mind at her lessons, and was too much for her temper. She and her friends were astonished at the difference in her when she went, at, I think, twelve years old, to stay for a month in a house where she had tea-breakfasts. She did, to be sure, cast very greedy looks at her cup of tea when it was coming; and she did make rather a voracious breakfast; but this was wearing off before the end of the month. She went home to her milk-breakfasts, her lump in the throat, and her morning depression of spirits and irritability. But at last the time came when she was tall enough to have tea with the older ones; and in a little while, she showed no signs of greediness, and thought no more about her breakfast than any body else.

I remember another case, where a similar mistake appeared more broadly still in its bad effects. In a family where it was the custom to have a great rice-pudding every Saturday, and sometimes also on the other baking day,—Wednesday,—there was a little fellow who hated rice. This was inconvenient. His mother neither liked to see him go without half his dinner, nor to provide a dish for him; for the child was disposed to be rather greedy, and troublesome with fancies about his eating. But in the case of the rice, the disgust was real, and so strong that it would have been better to let it alone. His mother, however, saw that it would be a benefit to him if he could get over it: and she took advantage of a strong desire he had for a book, to help him over his difficulty. The little fellow saw at a shop-window a copy of the Seven Champions of Christendom, with a gay picture of the dragon and St. George: and his longing for this little book was of that raging sort which I suppose only children ever feel. He was to have this book if he would eat rice-pudding. He eagerly promised; feeling at the moment, I dare say, when there was no rice within sight, as if he could live upon it all his days, to get what he wanted. When Saturday came, I watched him. I saw how his gorge rose at the sight of the pudding: but he fixed his eyes upon the opposite wall, gulped down large spoonfuls, wiped his mouth with disgust, and sighed when he had done, demanded his fee, ran for the book, and alas! had finished it, and got almost tired of it, before bedtime. The worst of it was,—he never again tasted rice. Here was the moral injury. He was perfectly aware that his bargain was to eat rice-pudding whenever it was upon table; and he meant to do it. But it required more fortitude than he could command when the desire for the book was gratified and gone: and his honour and conscience were hurt. Another bad consequence of this mistake about two or three of his dislikes was that he thought too much about eating and drinking; was dainty in picking his meat, and selfish about asking for the last bit, or the last but one, of any thing good. Of course, I do not speak in censure, when I give such anecdotes. I blame nobody where nobody meant any harm. On the one side there was a mistake; and it was followed by its inevitable consequences on the other.

In such a case, where there is a large family, with a plain common table, I should think the best way is for a child in ordinary health to take his chance. If there is enough of meat, potatoes, and bread to make a meal of, he may very well go without pudding, and should, on no account, have one provided expressly for himself: but he should be allowed to refuse it without remark. Where the mother can, without expense and too much inconvenience, consider the likings and dislikes of her children in a silent way, her kindness will induce her to do it: but it must be in a quiet way, or she will lead them to think too much about the thing; and to suppose that she thinks it an important matter.

This affair of the table is one worth a good deal of attention, as it regards the temper and manners of the household, and the personal habits of each. There is no reason why the father's likings as to food should not be seen to be cared for. If he is a selfish eater, he will ensure that the matter is duly attended to. If he is above such care for himself,—if it is clear that his pleasure at his meals is in having his family about him,—that is a case in which the mother need not conceal her desire to provide what is liked best. The father, who never asks or thinks about what is for dinner, is most likely to be the one to find before him what he particularly relishes; a dish cooked, perhaps, by his wife's or his little daughter's hands. And, again, if the little daughters see that their mother never thinks about her own likings, perhaps they will put in a word on market-day, or at such times, to remind her that somebody cares for her tastes. Then, again, in middle-class families, where the servants dine after the family, they should always be openly considered. After the pudding has been helped round once, and some quick eaters are ready for a second plateful, it must be an understood thing that enough is to be left for the servants.—On the ground of the danger of causing too much thought about eating and drinking, it is desirable that, where the family take their meals together, all should fare alike. If there is anything at table which the younger children ought not to have, it is better that they should, if possible, dine by themselves. This is the plan in great houses, where the little ones dine at one o'clock, eating freely and without controversy of what is on the table, because there is nothing there that can hurt them. If the family dine together, and there are two or more dishes of meat on the table at the same time, all must learn the good manners of dividing their choice, so that the father may not have to send a helping of goose to everybody, while none is left for himself, but that the mother's boiled mutton may have left half the goose for the choice of the parents. All this is clear enough: but, if a present arrives of anything nice,—oysters, or salmon, or oranges, or such good things as relations and friends often send to each other, it seems best for all the household to enjoy the treat together, who are old enough to relish it.

It can scarcely be necessary to mention that the earliest time is the best for training children to proper behaviour at table, as every where else. Every one of them has to be trained; for how are the little things to know, unless they are taught, that they are not to put their fingers in their plates, or to drain their mugs, or to make shapes with their potato, or to crumble their bread, or to kick their chairs, or to run away to the window before dinner is done? They will require but little teaching, if they see everybody about them sitting and eating properly; but it is hard upon children when they have been allowed to take liberties and be rude at the nursery dinner, and then have everything to learn, under painful constraint, as they are growing up.

I have been sometimes struck with the conviction that the bad manners I have seen at the school-room table arise from a misconception as to what dinner is. In one house, you see the busy father hurry from his work to table, hardly stopping to wash his hands, turning over to his wife the task of helping the children, or even pushing round the dish for them to help themselves,—throwing his dinner down his throat, and after it his solitary pint of porter; snatching his hat, and off again to business, almost without saying "good bye" to any one. When he is gone, the others think they have liberty to do as they please; and a pretty scene of confusion there is,—one child scraping a dish, another kneeling on a chair to reach over for something, a third at the window: and the mother with baby on her arm, coming at last to carry off the dishes, saying that she is sure dinner has been about quite long enough, while some of the children are perhaps really wanting more.—Again: one sees in a rich gentleman's family, ill-managed, a great mistake as to dinner. The bell is rung at the nominal dinner-hour,—or probably a good deal after it: for servants can hardly be punctual under such management. The soup is on the table, and one or two of the family are in their seats, waiting for the rest. One young lady has her fancy-work in her hand: another has the newspaper. Papa comes in for luncheon. He will have a plate of soup. The reader jumps up to help him; but the soup is cold. As nobody seems to wish for any cold soup, it is sent away; but turned back at the door by a hungry boy, who has only just learned that dinner is ready, and is ravenous for the first thing he can get to eat. While the joint is helped, one drops in from the stable,—another from the music-lesson; a third from botanising in the wood; and the first comers run away to look for something in the library, or to have a turn on the gravel walk, saying that they do not care for pudding, and will come back for cheese. Altogether, it is an hour and a half before the cloth is removed, and the weary governess can get her charge in order for the Italian master,—if indeed he be not come and gone in the interval. This is an extreme, but not an impossible case: and in such a case, the plea we shall hear is that it is a waste of time for a whole family to sit doing nothing but eating their dinners in the middle of the day: and that formality makes eating of too much importance. Such is the plea; and here lies the mistake. The object of dinner is not only eating but sociable rest. The dinner hour is a seasonable pause amidst the hurry of the busy day; and the harder people have to work, the completer should be the pause of the dinner hour. The arrangement is very important to health; for the largest meal of the day is best digested when it is eaten with regularity, at leisure, and in a cheerful mood of mind; and when a space of cheerful leisure is left after it. And more important still is the arrangement to the manners and tempers and dispositions of the family. It is a great thing that every member of a household should be habituated to meet the rest in the middle of the day, neatly dressed and refreshed;—the boys' coats brushed, and the girls' frocks changed or set straight; the hair smoothed, and face and hands just washed. It is a great thing that they should take their chief nourishment of the day in the midst of the most cheerful conversation, and at a time so set apart as that nobody is hankering after doing anything else. When we consider too that after dinner is the only time between Sunday and Sunday that the working father has for play with his infants,—who are in their beds, or too sleepy for fun, when he comes home in the evening,—we shall own that there is no waste of time in the dinner hour, even if nothing whatever is done but eating and talking. In fact, it is this time which, from its importance, ought to be saved from all encroachment. The washed faces, and the cloth on the table, and the hot dinner should all be in readiness when the father appears. Not a minute of his precious hour should be lost or spoiled by any one's unpunctuality, or any body's ill-manners. All should go smoothly at his table by every one's gentleness and cheerfulness and good-breeding. When the meal is finished, all the clearing away should be quickly and quietly done, that he may have yet a clear half-hour for rest, or for play with the little ones. Where this hour is managed as it ought to be,—(and nothing is easier under the care of a sensible mother) the busy father goes forth to his work again with his mind even more refreshed by his hour of cheerful rest than his body is strengthened by food.

On the remaining topic of Personal Habits,—Modesty,—Decency—it cannot be necessary to say much. The points of mistake which strike me the most are two:—I think that in almost every part of the world, people herd too much and too continually together:—and I think that few people are aware how early it is right to respect the modesty of an infant.

As to the first point;—it is one of the heaviest misfortunes of our country,—I speak advisedly,—that among whole classes of our people, poverty or want of space from other causes, compels them to herd together in crowds, night and day. No words are needed to show how little hope of health there can be when people live in this way; and even less hope of good morals. Among classes more favoured than these, it appears that there is little thought of making the provision that might easily be made for more privacy than people are yet accustomed to. I fear it is the wish that is wanting: for "where there's a will there's a way;" and I have been in many houses, both at home and abroad, where the requisite privacy might have been had, if any wish for it had existed. In the factory villages in the United States, I was painfully struck by this. I saw good and pretty houses built from the savings of the factory girls,—with their shady green blinds, and their charming piazzas without; and places within for book-shelves, piano and pictures and work-tables; but not a corner of any house was there where any young woman of the household could sit by herself for ten minutes in a day, or say her prayers, or wash. The beds were ranged in dormitories; or four or six in a room: and there were not even washing-closets. Here, there was no excuse of inability; and at home I too often see the same thing, where there is no sufficient excuse of inability.

Where each child cannot possibly have a room, or the use of a dressing-closet to itself, arrangements may easily be made, by having folding screens, to secure absolute privacy to every member of a household, for purposes of the mind, as well as the body. When I see how indispensable it is to the anxious and hard-worked governess to have a room to herself, and how earnestly she (very properly) insists upon it, I am always sorry when I remember how many have to go without this comfort,—which should be considered a necessity of life. When I think of the school-boy, with his burden of school cares upon him, and the young girl, thoughtful, anxious and irritable, as most people are, at times, in entering upon the realities of life; and of the wearied servant maid, and of the child in the first fervours of his self-kindling piety, I pity them if they have no place which they can call their own, for ever so short a time in the day, where they can be free from the consciousness of eyes being upon them. The thing may be done. Mrs. Taylor of Ongar, the wife of a dissenting minister, and mother of a large family, who from an early age worked for their bread,—did contrive, by giving her mind to it, to manage separate sleeping places for a wonderful number of her children; and, where this could not possibly be accomplished for all, she so arranged closets and hours as that every one could have his or her season of retirement, secure from disturbance.

As for the case of the infant, to which I alluded above,—I believe it to be this. The natural modesty of every human being may be left to take care of itself; if only we are careful that it is really left entirely free. It is the simplest matter in the world for the mother to give this modesty its earliest direction during the first weeks, months, and year or two of life. After that, it will not fail, if only it be duly respected. That this respect should begin very early is desirable, not because the innocent little creature has then any consciousness which can be injured by anything it sees or is allowed to do; but because as it grows up, it should be unable ever to remember the time when every thing was not arranged with the same modesty and decorum as at a later period. Again, in order to the preservation of true modesty, the smallest possible amount of thought should be bestowed upon it. All transactions, personal and domestic, should go on with the smoothness of perfect regularity, propriety, and consequent freedom of mind and ease of manners. And it conduces much to this that there should never have been a time when the child was conscious of any particular change in its management. It should never have seen much of any body's personal cares; and the more gradually it slides into the care of its own person, with its accompanying privacy, the better is the chance that it will not dwell on such matters at all, but have its mind free for other subjects, wearing its modesty as unconsciously as it carries the expression of the eye, or utters the tones of its voice.

# CHAPTER XXV.

## CARE OF THE HABITS.—FAMILY HABITS.

It is difficult to keep a distinction between personal and family habits. In our last chapter, on Personal Habits, we got to the family dinner table; and here, in speaking of Family Habits, we shall doubtless fall in with the characteristics of individuals.

First; as to occupations. Unless I knew for what class of readers I was writing this, it is difficult to assume what their occupations may be. In one class, the father may be busy in his office; and the mother in ordering a large household, taking care of the poor in her neighbourhood, and in study or keeping up her accomplishments; while the boys are with their tutor, and the girls with their governess, and the infants in the nursery.—In another, the mother may be instructing her girls, while busy at her needle; and the boys may be at a day-school, and the father in his warehouse or shop.—And again, this may be read by parents who cannot spare their children from home, because they keep no servants, and who charge themselves with teaching their young people, in such hours as can be spared from the actual business of living. One thing, however, is common to all these; and it is enough to proceed upon. All these are occupied. They have all business to do which ought to engage their faculties, regularly and diligently: so that the great principles and rules of family morals cannot fail to apply.

The first great point concerns them all equally:—Economy of Time. Nobody yet ever had too much time; and the rich need all they can save of it as much as the poorest. And the methods by which time is to be made the most of are universally the same. This seems to be everywhere felt, except among the ignorant. The most remarkable care, as to punctuality, is actually found, in our country, among the highest classes. It has bean said that "punctuality is the politeness of the great:" and so it is. It shows their consideration for other people's time and convenience: but there is more in it than that. The Queen, who is extraordinarily punctual, and statesmen, and landed-proprietors, and all who bear a burden of very important duty, are more sensible than those who have less responsibility of the mischief of wasting minutes which are all wanted for business; and yet more, of the waste of energy and freedom of thought, and of composure and serenity which are caused by failures in punctuality. For my own part, I acknowledge that not only is any compulsory loss of time the trial, of all little trials, that I most dislike, but that nothing whatever so chafes my temper as failure in punctuality in those with whom I have transactions. And to me, one of the charms of intercourse with enlightened and high-bred people is their reliableness in regard to all engagements, and their exact economy of time. To go from a disorderly household where no one seems to have any time, and where one has to try hard all day long to keep one's temper, to a great man's house, where half a hundred people move about their business as if they were one; where all is quiet and freedom and leisure, as if the business of life went on of itself, leaving minds at liberty for other work, is one of the most striking contrasts I have met with in society. And I have seen the same order and punctuality prevail, with much the same effect, in very humble households, where, instead of a score or two of servants, there were a few well-trained children to do the work. It is a thing which does not depend on wealth, but on intelligence. There is, (here and there, but not often) a great house to be seen where you cannot get anything you want till you have rung half-a-dozen times, and waited half an hour; where you are pretty sure to leave some of your luggage behind you, or be too late for the train, without any fault of your own; and where the meals, notwithstanding all the good cookery, are comfortless, from the restlessness and uncertainty of family and guests, and the natural discouragement of the servants. And there are houses of four rooms, where all goes smoothly from the politeness which arises from intelligence and affectionate consideration. When a new Administration came into office, some years ago, the Ministers agreed that not one of them should ever be waited for, on any occasion of meeting. At the first Cabinet dinner, the party went to table as the clock finished striking, though the Prime Minister had not arrived. The Prime Minister was only half a minute late; but he apologised, as for an offence against good manners. What would be thought of this in homes where the young people come dropping down to breakfast when their parents have half done, or where father or mother keeps the children fretting and worrying because they are waiting for breakfast when they ought to be about their morning business!

It may be said that the fretting and worrying are the greater offence of the two: and this is very true. So much the worse for the unpunctuality which causes a greater sin than itself. Why be subject to either? If a young person, no longer manageable as a child, continues, after all reasonable methods have been tried, to annoy his family by a habit of wasting his own time and theirs, there is no use in losing temper about it. Scolding and fretfulness will not bring him round, if other methods have failed. He must be borne with (though by no means indulged) and pitied as the slave of a bad habit. But how much better to avoid any such necessity! And it might always be avoided.

The way in which people usually fall into unpunctual habits is, I think, from interest in what they are about, whether it be dreaming in bed, or enjoying a walk, or translating a difficult passage, or finishing a button-hole in a shirt, or writing a postscript to a letter. In households where punctuality is really a principle, it should be a truth ever before all eyes that whatever each individual is about is of less importance than respect to the whole family. In a school, when the bell rings, one girl leaves off in the middle of a bar of music, another at the middle line of a repetition, and a third when she is within two figures of the end of her sum. The time and temper of mistress and companions must be respected first, and these things finished afterwards. And so it is in a well ordered household. The parents sacrifice their immediate interest in what they are about; and so must the children. And so they will, and with ease, when the thing is made an invariable habit, from the earliest time they can remember.

It is this punctuality, this undeviating regularity which is the greatest advantage that school has over home education, in regard to study. In a large family, where there is much business of living and few servants, it really is very difficult to secure quiet and regularity for the children's lessons. It seems at any one moment, of less importance that the sum should be done, and the verb conjugated, just for that once, than that the boy should run an errand, or the girl hold the baby. Now this will never do: and the small progress in learning usually made by the home-taught shows that it does not answer. The consideration is not of the particular sum, or practice in saying the verb, but of the habit of the children's minds. It is of consequence in itself that sums should be done and verbs learned in their proper season, because they cannot be so easily mastered afterwards; and there is plenty to be done afterwards; but much more important is it that the children should acquire that punctuality of faculties which grows out of punctuality of habits: and this can never be when there is any uncertainty or insecurity about the inviolability of their lesson-time. I know how difficult it is to manage this point, and how very hard it is for the mother to resist each day's temptation, if she has not fortified herself by system and arrangement, and by keeping constantly before her mind that nothing that her children can do by being called off from their books can be so important as what they sacrifice at every interruption. If it is possible for her to find any corner of the house where they may be undisturbed, and any hour of the day when she will allow no person whatever to call off her attention from them, she may do them something like justice: but she never can, though the books and slates may be about all the morning, if she admits any neighbour, or allows any interruption whatever. If possible, she will fix upon an hour when she may settle down with her plain-sewing, which requires no attention; and when her neighbours all know that they will not be admitted. One single hour, diligently employed, may effect a great deal. And it need not be all that the children give to study, though it be all that she can spare. They may learn at some other time in the day the lessons which she is to hear during the hour: and in that case, she must see that they are protected in their time of learning, as well as of repeating their lessons. Whether they are in their own rooms, or in the common sitting room, or she can spare any place for a school room, she must see that they have their minds to themselves, to do their business properly. If the father relieves her of the teaching, and hears the lessons at night, she will see more reason than ever for doing all she can to facilitate their being well learned.

If the time for lessons be necessarily but one hour in the day, let not the parents be uneasy, however much they might wish that their children should have their six hours of study, like those of richer people. Perhaps they can give both boys and girls educational advantages which those of the rich have not;—advantages which offer themselves in the natural course of humble life. I have witnessed a process of education for boys in a middle-class home which could not well be instituted in a great house, and among a multitude of servants, but which was of extraordinary benefit to the lads who were made happy by it. Their father gave into their charge some of the departments of the comforts of the house. One had charge of the gas-pipes and lamps. He was responsible for their good condition; and he was paid the same sum per annum that supervision by a workman would have cost. Another had charge of the locks and keys, the door-handles, sash-lines and window-bolts, bells and bell-wires: and he was paid in the same manner. Each had his workbench and tools in a convenient place; and, if every part of his province was always in order, so that there were no expensive repairs, he had some money left over,—which was usually spent in buying materials for mechanical handiworks. These lads were happier than poor Louis XVI. of France, who was so fond of making locks that he had a complete locksmith's workshop fitted up in a retired part of his palace: and delighted to spend there every hour that he could command. He was obliged to conceal his pursuit, both from the absurdity and the uselessness of it in his position; while these lads had at once the gratification of their faculties, and the dignity of usefulness. There are many offices about every house which may well be confided to boys, if they are intelligent and trustworthy;—that is, well educated up to the point required; and the filling of such offices faithfully is in itself as good a process of education as need be wished.

There is no need to declare the same thing about girls; for I suppose nobody questions it. I go further than most persons, I believe, however, in desiring thorough practice in domestic occupations, from an early age, for girls. I do not see why the natural desire and the natural faculty for housewifery which I think I see in every girl I meet, should be baffled because her parents are rich enough to have servants to do and to superintend everything about the house. If there was a king who could not help being a locksmith, I know of a countess who could not help being a sempstress. She made piles of plain linen, just for the pleasure of the work, and gave them away to her friends. Now, it is a very serious thing to baffle natural desires and abilities so strong as these, on account of mere external fortunes. If a girl of any rank has the economic faculties strong, it is hard upon her that they may not find their natural exercise in a direction,—that of household care,—which is appropriate to every woman, be she who she may; and if these faculties are less strong than they are usually found to be in girls, there is the more reason that they should be well exercised, as far as they will go.

I am sure that some,—perhaps most,—girls have a keener relish of household drudgery than of almost any pleasure that could be offered them. They positively like making beds, making fires, laying the cloth and washing up crockery, baking bread, preserving fruit, clear-starching and ironing. And why in the world should they not do it? Why should not the little lady have her little ironing box, and undertake the ironing of the pocket-handkerchiefs? I used to do this; and I am sure it gave me a great deal of pleasure, and did me nothing but good.—On washing and ironing days, in houses of the middle class, where all the servants are wanted in the wash-house or laundry, why should not the children do the service of the day? It will be a treat to them to lay the breakfast cloth, and bring up the butter from the cellar, and toast the bread; and, when breakfast is over, to put everything in its place again, and wash the china, and rub and polish the trays. They may do the same again at dinner; and while the servants are at meals, they may carry on the ironing in the laundry. And afterwards, there comes that capital exercise of sense and patience and skill,—the stocking-darning, which, done properly, is a much higher exercise than many people suppose. And when visitors come, why should not the girls have the chief pleasure which "company" gives to them,—the making the custard and the tarts, dishing up the fruit, and bringing out the best table linen? And what little girl is there in a market town who does not like going to market with her father or her mother, till she can be trusted to go by herself? Does she not like seeing the butcher's cleverness in cutting off what is wanted; and trying to guess the weight of joints by the look; and admiring the fresh butter, and the array of fowls, and the heaps of eggs, and the piles of vegetables and fruit? I believe it is no small treat to a girl to jump up early on the market-day morning, and reckon on the sight she is going to see. The anxiety may be great when she begins to be the family purchaser: but it is a proud office too; and when the first shyness is over, there is much variety and pleasantness in it.

By all means, as I have said, let the girls' economic faculties take the household direction, if they point that way, whatever be their fortunes and expectations. It can never do any woman harm to know, in the only perfect way, by experience, how domestic affairs should be managed. But, when the thing is done at all, let it be well done. Let the girl be really taught, and not suffered to blunder her way through, in a manner which could not be allowed in regard to anything taught as a lesson. One reason why girls know so much less than they should do, and so much less than they wish to do about household affairs, is that justice is not done them by proper teaching. The daughters of the opulent are at school, and have no opportunity of learning till they are too old to begin properly: but the case of middle and lower class girls is hardly better. When the mother is hurried, it is easier to do a thing herself than to teach, or wait for, an inexperienced hand: but a girl will never learn, if her enterprise is taken out of her hand at the critical moment. Nothing is more easily learned, or more sure to be remembered than the household processes that come under the hands of women: but then, they must be first clearly understood and carried through. Here then, the mother must have a little patience. She must bear to see a batch of bread or pastry spoiled, or muslins ironed wrong side out, or a custard "broke," or a loin of mutton mistaken for the neck, a few times over, and much awkwardness and slowness shown, before her little daughters become trusty handmaids. But, if she be a true mother, she will smile at this; and the father will not be put out if the pie is burned on one side, or the bread baked too quick, if he is told that this is a first trial by a new hand. He will say what he can that is encouraging, and hope for a perfect pie or loaf next time.

I believe it is now generally agreed, among those who know best, that the practice of sewing has been carried much too far for health, even in houses where there is no poverty or pressure of any kind. No one can well be more fond of sewing than I am; and few, except professional sempstresses, have done more of it: and my testimony is that it is a most hurtful occupation, except where great moderation is observed. I think it is not so much the sitting and stooping posture as the incessant monotonous action and position of the arms, that causes such wear and tear. Whatever it may be, there is something in prolonged sewing which is remarkably exhausting to the strength, and irritating beyond endurance to the nerves. This is only where sewing is almost the only employment, or is carried on for several hours together. When girls are not so fond of sewing as I was in my youth, and use the needle only as girls usually do, there is no cause for particular anxiety: but the mother should carefully vary the occupations of a girl disposed to be sedentary. If pleasant reading or conversation can go on the while, it is well. The family meals too, and other interruptions, will break off the employment, probably, before it has gone too far. But, if there is the slightest sign of that nervous distress called "the fidgets" (which truly deserves the name of "distress") or any paleness of countenance, lowness of spirits, or irritability of temper, there is reason to suppose that the needle has been plied too far; and, however unwilling the girl may be to leave work which she is bent upon finishing, it is clearly time that she was in the open air, or playing with the baby, or about some stirring business in the house. I have always had a strong persuasion that the greater part of the sewing done in the world will ere long be done by machinery. It appears much more easy than many things that are done by machinery now; and when it is considered how many minute stitches go to the making of a garment, it seems strange that some less laborious and slow method of making joins and edges has not been invented before this. Surely it will be done in the course of a few generations; and a great blessing the change will be to women, who must, by that time, have gained admission to many occupations now kept from them by men, through which they may earn a maintenance more usefully and with less sacrifice of health than by the present toils of the sempstress. The progress made in spinning, weaving, and especially knitting by machinery, and in making water-proof cloaks and other covering without the help of the needle, seems to point with certainty to an approaching time when the needle will be almost superseded. With this, and the consequent saving of time, must come a greater abundance of clothing, and an accompanying cheapness, which will be a great blessing to a large class by whom good and sufficient clothing cannot now be obtained. Meantime, our ways are improved, by the turning over of some of the work to machinery. The sewing-schools to which young ladies were sent in the last century, to sit six hours a-day on hard benches, too high for their feet to touch the ground, compelled to hold themselves upright, and yet to pore over fine cambric and linen, to do microscopic marking and stitching, are heard of no more. In their day, they bent many spines, spoiled many eyes, and plagued many a young creature with back-ache for life; so we may rejoice that they are gone, and must take care that none of their mischief is done at home, while all really useful good sewing can very easily be taught there.

One change which has taken place in our society since the peace has struck me much. Since the continent was opened to us, almost all who can afford to travel, more or less, have been abroad. Struck with the advantages to themselves of having their minds opened and enlarged by intercourse with foreign nations, and by access to foreign literature, art, and methods of education in some respects superior to our own, they have naturally desired to give such advantages to their children, while they were yet young enough to benefit fully by them. Great numbers of children, and young people yet growing, have been carried abroad by their parents, and, of course, have obtained more or less of the "advantages" for which they went. But at what cost? In my opinion, at a fatal one. Much might be said of the danger to health and life of a complete change of diet and habits at so early an age. A friend of mine was telling me, and I was agreeing with her, that she and I hardly know of a family of children who have travelled abroad for any length of time that has not been fatally visited with the dreadful bilious fever which, when it spares life, too often does some irreparable injury to the frame,—to brain, or sense, or limbs. Bad as this is, it is not the worst. The practice is against Nature; and those who adopt it must bear the retribution for offences against Nature's laws. Nature ordains a kind of vegetative existence for children till the frame is complete, and strengthened in its completeness. The utmost regularity of habits (which by no means implies dulness of life) produces, beyond all question, the most healthy frames, and there cannot be a sadder mistake than to suppose that any greater variety than the most ordinary life affords is necessary to the quickening or entertainment of a child's faculties. Life, with all its objects, is new to him. Its commonest incidents are deeply interesting to him. Birth and death are exciting to him, and solemn beyond expression. The opening and close of the seasons, and their varying pleasures and pursuits, the changes in the lives of the people about him; the evolution of his own little history,—the expanding of his faculties, his achievements in study, his entrance upon more and more advanced duties and intercourses;—these are enough to keep his mind in full life and vigour: and he cannot> receive his experience of life into the depths of his being unless he is at rest. If he is to commune with his own heart, he must be still. If he is to gather into his mind ripe observations of nature and man, and to store them up reflectively, he must be still. If his sentiments and emotions are to be the natural result of the workings of life upon him, he must be still, that life may work upon him undisturbed. I have devoted a close attention to this subject; and I certainly conclude, from my own observation, that the intellectual and moral value of families who have lived quietly at home (with due educational assistance) very far transcends that of young people whose anxious parents have dragged them about the world,—catching at advantages here and advantages there, unconscious of the sacrifice of the greatest advantage of all,—a natural method of life, with the quietude which belongs to it. I think that the untravelled have a deeper reflectiveness than the travelled,—a deeper sensibility,—a better working power, on the whole,—a better preparation for the life before them. They have more prejudice, and, of course, less accomplishment than the travelled; but life and years are pretty sure to abate the prejudice; and a better timed travel may give the accomplishment. If not, however,—if there must be a choice of good and evil at the outset of life, who would not rather see the fault of narrowness than of shallowness? A mind which has depth must, in ordinary course, widen; while a shallow mind, however wide, can never be worth much. In the sensibility, the difference is as marked as in the understanding: and no wonder; for to the quiet dweller at home life is an awful scroll, slowly and steadily unrolling to disclose its characters of fire, which burn themselves in upon the brain; while, to the young rover, life is but too much like a show-box, whose scenes shift too fast, and with too little interval, to make much impression. I mention this here, chiefly for the sake of parents who may feel occasional regrets that they cannot give to their children what they suppose to be the "advantages" of travel. My conviction is that their children are happier than they suppose. A moment's thought will show them how few the rovers can be,—how overwhelming must be the majority of those who must stay at home: and we may always be confident that the lot of the great majority, duly improved, must be sufficient for all the purposes of human life. Nothing that I have said is meant at all in disapprobation of those occasional changes of scene and society which all young people require more or less. On the contrary, I would indicate, as one of the advantages of a regular home life, that it prepares the novice to profit the more by such occasional changes. It is a magnificent event in the life of a quiet, industrious family when a house-painting, or other domestic necessity, authorises a visit to the sea-side, or a plunge into the country for a couple of months. It serves as a prodigious stimulus to the intellect; and the recollection never loses its brilliancy, to the latest period of life. It is worth more to novices than a whole year of continental travelling to practised rovers. The sunsets have sunk deep. The light-house, the dip in the waves, the shingle, the distant fleet—or the gorse on the common, the wood paths, with their wild flowers, the breezy down, the cottage in the lane,—call up a thrill in the heart of the town-bred child whenever the images are called up. Such changes are good; but they are not roving in search of "advantages." Again, when one child among several appears to pine in any degree, becomes irritable or depressed, looks pale, or ceases to grow, it is a sign that some change is needed. If such a boy or girl should be invited by some relation or friend on a visit of any length, it is probable that all will come right. The mind wants an airing, perhaps; and in a fresh abode, among new objects, and kind friends, and different companionship, and change of habits, without any further excitement, brooding thoughts are dispersed, domestic affections revive and strengthen, the mind overflows with new ideas, and after a time, home becomes intensely longed for; and the young absentee returns home—to father's greeting, and mother's side, and brothers and sisters' companionship, with more rapture than the prospect of the journey ever caused. Such a change as this is good; but it is not roving for educational "advantages." It is an agreeable tonic medicine; not a regimen of high diet.

The case of the only child seems to ask a word of kindness here. At the best, the case of the only child is a somewhat mournful one,—somewhat forlorn,—because it is unnatural. If it is unnatural for a multitude of children of the same age to herd together in an Infant school, it is at least as much so for a little creature to live alone among people with full-grown brains, and all occupied with the pursuits and interests of mature life. It is very well for the father to romp with his child at spare times, and for the mother to love it with her whole heart, and sympathise with it, with all the sympathy that such love can inspire. This is all well: but it does not make them children,—nor, therefore, natural companions for a child. In this case, above all others, it is desirable that the child should be sent to school, when old enough: and especially if the only one be a boy. A good day school, where play is included, may do much to obviate the disadvantages of the position. If this cannot be done, it is really hardly to be hoped that mischief will not be done on the one side or the other,—of too much or too little attention and sympathy. Some may wonder at the idea of the only child being in danger of having too little sympathy from its parents: but such cases are very conceivable and are occasionally witnessed. If everybody sees how an only child,—the light and charm of the house, the idol of the mother, and the pet of everybody, must unavoidably become of too much importance in its own eyes, and suffer accordingly,—who should feel this so anxiously and constantly as the conscientious parents of an only child? and what is more probable than that, in their anxiety not to spoil the mind they have under their charge, they should carry the bracing system somewhat too far, and depress the child by giving it less fostering and sympathy than it needs? They would not, for its own sake, have it troublesome to their friends, or self-important, or selfish; and they keep it back. But alas! if put back, the little thing is driven into loneliness; and children are not made for loneliness, in any but a desert life. Give a child the desert to rove in, with brown sheep to tend, and a young camel to play with, and rocks and weeds, and springs and stars and shrubby palms to live amongst, and he may make a very pleasant life of it, all alone; but not if he lives in a street, and must not go out alone, and passes his life among square rooms and stair-cases, and the measured movements of grown-up people. An only child must be troublesome, as long as he is a child. He craves play, and sympathy, and constant companionship: and he cannot do without them—he must not be required to do without them. If he is not sent to school, grown people must be his companions and playfellows,—the victims to his restlessness; and he must be troublesome.—The case is nearly the same,—only somewhat less desperate,—with a girl. Her parents cannot, if they have eyes, hearts, or consciences, see her pine. They must either provide her with natural companionship, or they must let themselves and their friends be appropriated by her as companions, till she grows up into fitness to be a companion to them.—It is not included in this necessity that there should be selfishness of temper and manners. The more fully and naturally the needs of the social nature are met and supplied, the less is the danger of this kind arising from peculiarity of position.

# CHAPTER XXVI.

## CONCLUSION.

Is there any other department of Household Education than those on which I have touched? No one can be more aware than I am of the scantiness of what I have said, when compared with the vastness of the range and of the importance of the subject. I could only, as I declared at the beginning, tell a little of what I have seen and thought of the training of families in private life: but, admitting the meagre character of the whole, is there any one department left untouched? I am not aware of any that could be treated of in a volume for general reading.

Some may, perhaps, ask for a chapter on Social Habits: and an important subject it truly is. But it appears to me to be included in that of Family Habits and Manners. The same simplicity and ingenuousness, the same respect and kindliness, the same earnestness and cheerfulness, which should pervade the conduct and manners in the interior of the household are the best elements of conduct and manners in the world. I see no discretion and no grace which is needed in wider social intercourses that is not required by those of home. To the parents there may be some anxiety and uneasiness when their sons and daughters make intimacies out of the house. The warm friendships of youth may not perhaps be such as the parents would have chosen. They may be such as surprise and disappoint the parents. But the very fact of the surprise and disappointment should show them that there is something more in the matter than they understand or should seek to control. They cannot control the sympathies of any one; and no one being can fully understand the affinities which exist between others. The points to be regarded are clear enough: and when the best is done that can be done, the rest may be left without anxiety.

The main point is to preserve the full confidence of the young people. If perfect openness and the utmost practicable sympathy be maintained, all must be safe. Young people must win their own experience. They must find out character for themselves: they must try their own ground in social life; they must be self-convicted of the prejudices and partialities which belong to their immaturity; and, while their own moral rectitude and their ingenuous confidence in their parents subsist, they can take no permanent harm from casual associations which may be far from wise. The parents should remember too how very important a part of the training of each individual is of a kind which the parents have nothing to do with but to witness, and to have patience with, as a piece of discipline to themselves.

As has been observed before, there seems to be a fine provision in human nature for rectifying home tendencies which would otherwise be too strong, and for supplying the imperfections of home experience by the process which takes place,—the revolution of moral tastes which ensues,—upon the introduction of young people into a wider circle than that of home. The parents have naturally,—unavoidably,—laid the most stress in the training of their children on those qualities which are strongest in themselves, and slight, more or less, such as they disregard, or are conscious of not excelling in themselves. When the young people go out into the world, they are struck by the novel beauty of virtues in full exercise which they have seen and heard but little of, and fall in love with them, and with those who possess them, and, with a fresh enthusiasm, cherish them in themselves. Thus it is that we so often see whole families of young people becoming characterised by the virtues in which their parents are most deficient; and also, as a consequence, by the faults which are the natural attendants of those virtues. I have seen a case of parents, indulgent and faithful to their children, virulently censorious to the rest of the world;—the children, while wearing pinafores, disgusting from their gleeful gossip, picked up from the elders, scorning and quizzing everybody's thoughts and ways;—and those same children, when abroad in the world as men and women, growing first grave,—then just and fair,—then philosophical, and at last indulgent, as the truly philosophical must ever be. They preserved the keen insight into character and the movements of mind in which they had been trained at home, after first recognising, and then opening their hearts to the beauty of charity. I have seen the children of imprudent, lavish, and embarrassed parents turn out eminently correct in their management of money matters:—the children of an untidy mother turn out perfectly methodical;—the children of a too social father, remarkably retired and domestic; and so on. Very often the new and late virtue becomes too prominent, excluding the hereditary opposite qualities; and in that case, when these young people become parents, the same process takes place, and their children strongly resemble their grandparents. It is a curious spectacle,—that of such a moral oscillation;—and it is so common that every one may observe it. One of the pieces of instruction that it yields is to parents;—that they must now let Nature work, and take off their hands from meddling. They may themselves learn something if they will, in silence and sympathy, from the spectacle of the expansion of their children; and they may take the lesson into a light and easy heart if they have hitherto done their duty as well as they know how. There is nothing in what they see to hurt any but an improper pride: and they may make sure of an increased reverence and love from their children if they have the magnanimity to go hand in hand with them into new fields of moral exercise and enterprise, and to admit the beauty and desirableness of what they see.

Here we have arrived at the ultimate stage of Household Education,—that where the entire household advances together, in equal companionship, towards the great object of human existence, the perfecting of each individual in it. We set out with the view that the education of a household comprehended the training and discipline of all its members; and here we find ourselves at the same point again, amidst a great difference in the circumstances. They are no longer all under the same roof. One may be in the distant town; another in a far country; a third in the next street, but seen only on Sundays: but still they are one Household company, living in full confidence and sympathy, though their eyes may seldom meet, and a clasp of the hand may be a rare luxury. The mother who once received discipline from her child when he was a wailing infant, keeping her from her rest at midnight, receives another discipline from him now when she sees him in earnest pursuit of some high and holy aim whose nobleness had become somewhat clouded to her through the cares of the world, and her very solicitude for him. The father who had suffered perhaps too keenly from some gross faults of his thoughtless boys in their season of turbulence, receives from them now a new discipline—a rebuke full of sweetness,—in the proof they offer that he had distrusted Nature,—had failed in faith that she would do her work well, if only the way was duly kept open for her. There is a new discipline for them in the gradual contraction of the family circle, in the deepening quietness of the house, and in the loss of the little hourly services which the elderly people now think they hardly valued enough while they had them every hour. We can never say that any part of the discipline of life is over for any one of us; and that of domestic life is certainly not over for affectionate parents whose children are called away from their side, however unquestionable the call may be.

As for the younger generation of the household,—their education by their parents never ceases while the parents live: and the less assertion the parents make of this, the deeper are the lessons they impress. The deepest impressions received in life are supposed to be those imparted to the sensitive and tenacious mind of childhood: but the mature reverence and affection of a manly mind are excited more efficaciously than the emotions of childhood can ever be when the active men and women who were once the children of a household see their grey-haired parents in the midst of them looking up to Nature, and reaching after Truth and Right with the humble trust and earnest docility which spread the sweetest charm of youth over the countenance of age. However many and however rich are the lessons they have learned from their parents, assuredly, in such a case, the richest is the last.

**THE END**

www.ingramcontent.com/pod-product-compliance
Lightning Source LLC
Chambersburg PA
CBHW081722100526
44591CB00016B/2466